SOLDIER ON

SOLDIER ON

An Autobiography by

Colonel Sir Mike Ansell

Foreword by

H.R.H. The Prince Philip,
Duke of Edinburgh

PETER DAVIES : LONDON

Peter Davies Ltd
15 Queen St, Mayfair, London W1X 8BE
London   Melbourne   Toronto
Johannesburg   Auckland

© 1973 by Colonel Sir Michael Ansell
First published 1973

Printed in Great Britain by
Richard Clay (The Chaucer Press) Ltd
Bungay, Suffolk

CONTENTS

ILLUSTRATIONS

————◆◆◆————

ACKNOWLEDGEMENTS

I wish to express my sincere thanks to my sister, Mrs Williams, to all my family and to some very close friends who have so encouraged and helped me with this book.

In particular I would like to say how grateful I am to Mr Denis Goacher, who has spent many hours editing and correcting my 'indifferent' English, and to Mr Ronald Duncan, without whose enthusiasm and advice, particularly in 1970, I would never have dared to complete this story. Also I wish to thank Miss Sally Doman, my secretary, who had endless typewriting to do, and finally Mr Ronald Attwood, who spent many an hour reading out loud to me.

Colonel Sir Mike Ansell
March 1973

FOREWORD

by

H.R.H. The Prince Philip,
Duke of Edinburgh

The happiest mortals are those who are consumed by an abiding passion. If that enthusiasm is combined with a talent for organisation, great things can be achieved.

Sir Michael Ansell's passion for anything to do with horses has carried him through more than a fair share of crises and disasters. His talent for organisation has lifted horse shows and equestrian sports to a remarkable level in this mechanical age.

Sir Michael tells his story with characteristic simplicity and directness and it is a story well worth reading.

PART ONE

I

Across the Divide

It is five o'clock in the morning. The wind rocks the candles in those chestnut trees, a white cat stalks by the flower border to the left of this window looking west; the first birds sing and clouds sweep over me and change. How do I know? Men say, and I am well aware, that I am blind. But memory and imagination tell me everything.

Like all people of my age, I've known three distinct 'worlds': pre-1914, *entre les deux guerres*, and post-1945. I come of an Army family, the first of which to attain notoriety was General Sir Thomas Picton, killed at Waterloo. My father inevitably set the pattern of my character in several crucial respects: he was a fine polo player, a terrific worker and commanded his regiment at the age of thirty-nine (which in 1911 was considered very young indeed). So I cannot remember a time when I was not filled with the urge to succeed, to excel. Many would say that I've had more than a glimpse of fame and glory; by contrast the iron balance of fate came down to make me simultaneously blind and a prisoner of war—the latter worse than death for a professional soldier—and I am twice a widower. Now as I sit in this house a friend has aptly named 'your cathedral', and which atom bombs and the Inland Revenue have so far mercifully spared, I often seek to conjure a meaning from these sixty-eight years. Let us go back to the beginning.

About 1909 I remember being at Mhow in Central India—how we got there I've no idea. My father commanded a squadron of the Inniskillings, and my sister Bunny and I both had our ponies: mine was Turnips, my sister's Carrots. I remember Turnips was at times rather stubborn, yet not only was I taught to ride but to drive—although I'm quite certain it was merely sitting *on* a pony and *in* the trap.

One day, when my father was recovering from enteric fever, we were allowed to pass the white sheet into his room and saw at the far end on a table two mysterious round objects wrapped in bright-coloured paper: allowed to take our pick, I grabbed and uncovered, a tortoise; Bunny, a melon—which needless to say we shared. For some reason this incident is engraved on my mind and seems obscurely significant.

3

Returned to England, my father was given command of the 5th Dragoon Guards in 1911. I know from what I've heard since that he had no easy task: the 5th Dragoons were not at this time at their best; he quickly got rid of several elderly, inefficient N.C.O.s and fairly smartened up the officers. The regiment had a strong Masonic Lodge, and this was not popular with my father, feeling, as he always did, you should not have two loyalties. He also believed that young officers should be spending money on hunting, shooting and polo rather than on what we'll call 'social activities'; he preached nothing he didn't do himself, so immediately became teetotal.

Even at that time he was certain there was going to be a war with Germany: therefore the regiment must be ready, the men able to ride and shoot superlatively, the horses fit and well trained. In 1912 they moved to Aldershot, and became the most efficient cavalry regiment to go to war in 1914. I remember the regiment's arrival at Aldershot, and how struck I was by the men marching up from the station, dressed in khaki and brass helmets without plumes—rather like the 'battle bowler' in years to come.

Determined to leave no idea or comparison hidden, my father went round the Cavalry School at Saumur and others in Italy and Belgium; his reports emphasised the poor standard of horsemastership on the Continent, for he was a great horsemaster, though oddly his methods were constantly under attack. There was a paper called *The Soldier* in which officers were freely criticised, and my father much maligned for casting out dead wood and giving accelerated promotion to the younger N.C.O.s; he was even reproached for turning all troop horses out in Farnham Park, during winter months, to save their forage allowance for training. An example of his thoroughness: on manœuvres a motor lorry followed the regiment, carrying a corn crusher used to bruise all the oats. That may seem trivial, but the point is that he was always thinking about the condition of the horses. Convinced that war with Germany would be inevitable, he knew that only a highly trained, efficient regiment could hope to keep down the loss of life.

Both my parents loved gardening, and all flowers—something I inherited from them—my father particularly fond of geraniums, roses, violas, and more than proud of his great tubs of strawberries: strawberries which even pushed through the sides where two-inch holes had been bored. Oh, the excitement when I discovered that my Christmas present was to be a set of gardening tools! These were hidden in a cupboard on the landing and when no one was about I rolled the carpet with a tremendous roller, dug and then raked, and somehow was never discovered.

Like most children, we were overwhelmed with joy and restlessness when the bicycles came, and we could ignore the ponies for a bit—though we dared not show this! I, especially, nearly suffocated in my efforts not to display too much interest in a mere bicycle. I suppose I learnt to enjoy football and cricket, though chess meant more to me—my father taught me that thoroughly. But, of course, my chief education was riding.

The Riding Master, a fat old gentleman by the name of Lang, who instructed much of the time on his feet with a long whip, was the last of the 'rankers' to hold this position, for it subsequently became the post of a Commissioned Officer. Sometimes we rode in the School emptied for raking and watering—too tempting for some of the staff, who just put the hose in the way of my pony, or one called Bogey French would dart out from behind a door. Gradually I was made to ride with the recruits, do everything they did, jumping, no reins or stirrups, and often had to demonstrate to them—who truthfully disliked riding as much as I. Occasionally, when I knew a sudden order to ride was coming, I crept into the upstairs lavatory and locked myself in until too late to obey the summons. Nevertheless I learnt: I learnt to ride, and to conceal my fears.

I also disliked boxing. Two or three times a week I reported to the Band-room, where Boy McCormick awaited me. He was twice my size and instructed not to hit me hard, but I found the blows were hard all the same. Whether I hit him by mistake, or whether the temptation to hit the Colonel's son was just too glorious, I never decided, but often I returned with red eyes, redder and bleeding nose, proud of the nose though not the eyes. I never made a boxer and never enjoyed it; Boy McCormick, on the other hand, won three Army titles in one night around 1920, and later became British Lightweight Champion.

In the mornings, while my father shaved, I used to go in and we played noughts and crosses without pencil or paper—I don't think I've ever since been beaten at this game. I was also bombarded with endless sums to add up in my head, which may have improved my memory. This was typical of my father's method: motor-cars were still 'kept in their place' (it was always a pony and trap), but occasionally when going a long way to polo we had a taxi, and I used to sit in front reading the map, which I honestly enjoyed, as my father used to make me feel important; and similarly at polo, I either held sticks or spare ponies. And so in these innumerable small ways he formed much of my character: he was stern, but never once beat me, nor do I remember his ever being really angry. Unyielding though: for example, I must never be late, and once when he was due to go to Cowdray he simply left me behind—punishment enough. On his return, he merely said, 'Don't be late again.'

One day, quite suddenly it seemed, this life of sailor-suits, riding, boxing and tales from the soldiery came to an end. I cannot even remember my first term at St Michael's, Westgate on Sea, so great was my misery, but the beginning of the second must have been nearly as bad. My father being away on manœuvres, I was met in London by Major and Mrs Peterkin and whipped off to the Cavalry Club for what everyone hoped might be an excellent luncheon—until I started to cry and complain of being very ill. Poor Mrs Peterkin thought I really *was* ill and despatched the Major to telephone. It was decided that I should spend that night at Wimbledon with the Peterkins, my father would return and come up next day with my sister Bunny *en route* for Miss Hare's (her school, also at Westgate). Next morning I'd made a miraculous recovery and off we went again to London to link up with my family. This time we did have an excellent lunch, at the Savoy. My father always liked lunching there because you could get an *hors d'œuvre* which cost half a crown, you could have as much as you liked, and that course was all he ever had. On this occasion he said he was sorry I'd felt ill, and wasn't in the least angry—but the cure was to come.

At Victoria, Bunny and I were handed over to Miss Hare, and I travelled with the complete girls' school in large reserved Pullmans. My arrival at Westgate had been expected for I was met by the Head Porter, a large man with an enormous grey moustache, a dark blue suit and a dark blue cap embroidered with ST MICHAEL'S. Bunny and the girls left one way, my friend the porter and I, the other. The headmaster's wife, Mrs Hawtrey, could not have been kinder, but there my happy reception ended—my friends had already learnt of my travelling companions from London. I don't think I've ever again been late returning from holidays, or leave, in my life. Oddly enough, I was once told that my father had no sympathy whatever for men or officers who came back from leave late, and no excuse of missed trains, fog or breakdown was accepted. If a man was late, he was late, and punished. Consequently men were not late. Years after, when I was adjutant to Roger Evans commanding in Aldershot, the habit of returning late from leave had grown and he introduced the same system; despite wintry difficulties, the whole regiment returned on time.

St Michael's, on the outskirts of Westgate, comprised a number of the ugliest Victorian villas imaginable; each villa joined by a corrugated passage-way, except where a gloomy, gas-lit tunnel took one under the road. The playing-field, bordered by either a main road or the railway, was totally lacking in character. We all had rooms to ourselves, though the larger ones were halved by wooden partitions. I found myself in the main villa with the Hawtreys and the youngest boys; Mrs Hawtrey tucked us up, and comforted us when necessary—very much so in my case, for I was desperately lonely and cried nearly every night at the beginning of that second term.

Mr Hawtrey, known as 'Beetle', looked exactly like one as he hobbled along on two sticks; this dear old gentleman always wore a morning-coat and mortar-board, except while coaching at cricket, when the mortar-board was exchanged for a top hat.

Other details of that time which stand out: trooping into Chapel after

6

breakfast, envious looks at the senior boy who worked the organ bellows, a much-coveted job. Football, wearing dark blue knickerbockers and dark blue stockings, shorts quite unheard of. Postal chess with my father: each morning I received his move, each day I sent a postcard with mine. Our books, of course, were G. A. Henty's. After Sunday luncheon, a long crocodile in our Eton suits and top hats. Until the longed-for summer holidays came—but this time they brought us war: 1914.

Immediately after mobilisation, reservists poured back in their hundreds, every man eager to be taken with the regiment. Two tests had to be fulfilled: (*a*) that you were a first-class shot and (*b*) capable of riding around a square jumping-lane, with arms folded, without stirrups.

Although only nine, I was made a cycle orderly, and all day sat on a bench outside the guard-room waiting to carry messages. I felt important, as my father intended.

The excitement was tremendous; those who hadn't been to war, not realising what it meant, were convinced it would be finished within a few months. My father knew and said it would be years. Desperately upset and serious, he became more and more taciturn. The barracks were one great hustle, stores and ammunition being drawn, the Full Dress Scarlet handed in—who realised it would never be issued again, that the days of a Cavalry Brigade galloping past in full dress were gone for ever? And then one, morning the mounted regiment paraded on the square at 4.00 a.m., and left to entrain at Aldershot. Very quiet the barracks, at breakfast, that morning.

So during those next weeks we waited for news, the odd letter which was really no news, the bleak printed cards saying, 'I am well, etc.' On a large map we stuck flags, marking the rapid retreat of the Allies. I can remember standing in the stable one day, my mother by the south wall of the housel when a telegraph boy came and my mother, I think, knew what was in the envelope. 'Regret to inform you that Lt-Col Ansell reported killed in action.'

How well did I know my father at the age of nine? I was frightened of him, yet he didn't show anger; he was severe—told to do something I did it quickly. Later, of course, I learnt much about him in the regiment: men recognised that he was almost inhumanly fair, always set an example, never asking anything of anybody that he would not do himself. He was one of those who used to say, 'There is no such word as can't.' Everyone admired him as a fine soldier and, more important, a great leader. No one can escape his fate, so it's useless to imagine what might have happened if war had been declared three months later, for he'd been ear-marked to succeed General Vaughan as Commandant of the Cavalry School at Netheravon.

He was killed, leading the regiment, on 1 September 1914, at the battle of Néry, a village close to the forest of Compiègne. There are many complete accounts of this battle, now considered a classic of cavalry action.

In the Army, the saying is, you 'follow the drum': you have little opportunity to make a home. Already, by nine years old, we'd moved about six times. Captain Vivian Williams, my father's equitation officer, then became our guardian, and Uncle Jim, who was in the Yeomanry, persuaded my mother to buy 'The Fields', Southam, in the middle of Warwickshire. Like Pillhead, where I'm sitting, it had a great tree which was part of the house—a huge cedar, far too generous with its shade but superb for our friends to climb (I say 'our friends' because I hated climbing, was much too frightened). An old pony of about fifteen hands, called Topthorne, had been got for me— but need I ride? I pleaded, I much preferred the bicycle. Wisely, my mother never goaded me.

There were changes at Westgate. I found I had to work, and that was made plain by the first birching. The Head Porter arrived in Mr Hawtrey's study with what looked like a birch broom: the noise it made was worse than the pain, blood drawn in a few places, but worst of all my mother found among extras on the bill: one birch, ten shillings. A very expensive besom.

At The Fields we had the most magnificent conservatory, unused, and there I deployed my lead soldiers, made or simulated trees, trenches, roads, rivers and railways, and with the current craze for Meccano I felt there was nothing I couldn't build.

The Boy Scout role I did enjoy, eventually becoming Leader of the Lion Patrol of the Southern Troop: I even played a bugle in the band, or more accurately, pretended to, only really holding it to my mouth. I can't think how I was never found out.

Also at this time my mother became keen on chickens, and unfortunately Bunny and I had to help clean out their large houses. I fear I have never liked chickens.

Meanwhile the school had been moved from Westgate. Out for a walk on the cliffs one day, we'd seen a small German plane chased by two British planes drop two or three bombs into the sea and then slowly fall in itself: enough to decide the new headmaster, Mr Cautley, that it was much too dangerous an area for such valuable offspring. So, to Surrenden in Kent, which had a lovely park full of deer and pheasants. It was let to an American, Walter Wynans, a character straight out of the Wild West: he was a brilliant shot and used to chase the deer in a trap, shooting with a long-barrelled pistol. Periodically there were crazes for doing War Work; during one of these we were divided into squads to collect wood for the boilers, those who gathered most receiving one of Mrs Cautley's eggs for tea. I and my lot soon discovered that small stuff, quickly broken up, made more bulk—and we regularly received one extra egg per week.

Then there were my endless bad reports: 'Could do better if he tried.' Mr Cautley had exchanged the birch for the slipper, but that hurt much more. I had the distinction of one prize only, a leaving prize. But 'the proof of the pudding, etc.', and when I came to sit for the Common Entrance to Wellington I passed easily, thirty-first out of about eighty. I'd come to love my life at Hawtrey's, as it was now called, having captained the cricket eleven, captained the Crusaders and won my hockey and soccer colours. But I never got higher than the second form.

2

Wellington, Sandhurst, India

I believe I went to Wellington in September 1918. For the first time I climbed to the Lynedoch dormitory, up landing after landing of stone steps with iron bars as banisters, right to the top. Fifteen to eighteen cubicles on either side, mine, of course, at the far end. I gazed into my new nest: an iron bedstead, a wooden table, a chair; under the bed, a jerry, a flat tin bath in which lay a tin can. At the bottom of the four flights of stone stairs was the only lavatory and an iron gate to lock us in at night. My mother was as shaken as I, we made a tender farewell, and I returned to sit with my luggage and review the position. There was another new man in the room opposite, and these were rightly the two worst-placed, for at the prefect's call 'Boyee!' all the juniors ran, and the last to arrive had to do the job.

At about nine that first evening we were told to get down to 'Swipes' if we wanted anything to eat. We drew a mug of very weak cocoa and two ship's biscuits—the war had not quite ended. Then to bed, deathly cold, and I dared not cry for fear of being heard.

Since I'd passed in fairly high, I found myself in the upper fourth, but I quickly discovered that there was absolutely no necessity to work. Reports were uniformly bad and eventually my poor mother wrote to Mr Cautley, who replied, 'Mike is certainly having an unholy loaf, surely some master must be man enough to make him work!' I soon found I liked Rugger and enjoyed running—which was just as well.

On November 11 the Armistice was signed, and the school went mad. All the wooden bars across our windows were smashed, the window-seat mattresses hurled into the quadrangle where eager boys waited to cut them open, until finally the bursar and four or five porters appeared on the roof with fire hoses. That night the whole College marched two miles up to the top of the ridges, where we lit an enormous bonfire.

This was the first of three dramas during my time at Wellington. Next came the 'flu epidemic about which one can hardly joke: in a matter of hours, five hundred boys were ill and had taken to their beds; there was no one to look after us; we just waited for mothers and elder sisters to come and take us home. After the Plague, the Great Fire, eighteen months later—we had a grandstand view from Lynedoch, as 'Anglesey' and 'Blucher' opposite us burnt like kindling wood. With seventy bedless boys and classrooms flooded, we thought delightedly we must be sent home, but at six o'clock the great bell tolled us to chapel, the firemen worked through the night, and next day all was normal.

Meantime, my mother had moved house yet again to 'Greenlands', a square squat place in about seven acres not far from Wellesbourne. There we had no ponies, but she became madly keen on goats, pigeons and rabbits—and particularly the last. We had every kind of blessed rabbit, according to whims of fashion: Chinchillas, Hanoverians and the attractive Dutch, Belgian Hares and the Flemish Giants of the double chins. I shall never forget that rabbitry on hot days when it was my job to water them. Ironically, at about this time my Uncle Jim started me shooting. I used to go to his place at Catthorpe and there I was armed with a sixteen-bore single-barrelled shot-gun and sent out with the keeper to shoot sitting rabbits!

I must have been about sixteen when I suddenly wished to start riding again. I'd been to stay in the Mess of the 5th Dragoon Guards stationed at Colchester; my guardian, 'Pudding' Williams, had been keeping an eye on me. One of my early meets was at Willoughby with the Warwickshire, and hounds ran close to my grandmother's house; I picked my own line and my horse jumped superbly. On the following Sunday we went there to luncheon, and afterwards a young gunner subaltern, Jock Campbell, showed my grand-mother a post and rails I'd jumped—apparently, unknown to me, nearly all the field had turned away. This incident gave me tremendous confidence, and I'm afraid that in all my hunting I've enjoyed setting the line and competing against friends. (Jock and I later became great friends and he as a Major-General won the Victoria Cross when leading his Armoured Division in the Desert.)

During term-time the pattern continued: little work, a lot of games. It had always been taken for granted that I would go into the Army but now, at about seventeen, I toyed with dreams of making money, and thought of becoming an engineer. I realise that unconsciously I was seeking to avoid the Army exam, but eventually I felt convinced that the Army it had to be. My French was appalling, so my mother arranged for me to stay with a person at Courseilles-sur-mer.

A bus dropped me in the village square on Joan of Arc's Day, and for that reason alone no one was in the least interested in my arrival. Somehow I found the Vicarage, full of children from Paris, and the place in total gloom for one of them had been drowned bathing that day. Bells tolled, and no one spoke. There was little point in being hungry for no one wished to cook, and for the next couple of days I took no part in that 'family life' which, miracu-lously steeping me in French, would enable me to soar through my examinations. When lessons did finally start one morning after the *café au lait*, my tutor' soon realised that I was unlikely to make any progress, and I realised, quite as soon, that I'd have much more fun if I could get out of the house immediately after breakfast. And so I did.

There as everywhere the tennis court was useful for more than exercise and I quickly found the most attractive tall fair French girl, who proved only too willing to learn English—instead of my learning French. In the evenings we danced at the casino, though how she put up with my dancing I cannot imagine. Presumably all could be endured for the English lesson. I had a few smart silk handkerchiefs, and slowly she got the lot as scarves.

Back at Wellington I worked desperately hard. I had to. When the Army exam came I felt I'd done not too badly and almost bounced up to London for my Orals in French and German. I remember nothing of the interviews, but I do remember staying at Brown's Hotel, for as my family was well known there I managed to put everything, including theatre tickets, on my mother's bill. Then, at Gorse House, Rugby (we'd moved once more), each morning we met the postman and searched every page of *The Times*, until one day when least expecting it, and looking almost casually, I saw I'd passed 70th out of 120.

And so to Sandhurst. I arrived there for the Summer term, which started in February, ending in July. There were only two terms, and at that time we did, in all, two years. I've often said that everything one does in life depends for success on 'timing'. Whether you ride a race, ask your wife for something, play tennis, cricket or whatever, if you're going to succeed, your timing must be right. It seems to be partly a matter of intuition or instinct, sometimes a dash of luck, occasionally an act of decision and will. My career was now set, this must be the time to work, and fortunately I did. I was very happy at Sandhurst, and I worked like the devil.

The first twelve weeks were drill, drill, then more drill: this element of military training is much criticised nowadays but I am still convinced it is the only way to ensure an invincible discipline—without which there's no hope of real efficiency. Nevertheless, when I can't sleep at night, I sometimes try to count how many times a day we had to change clothes for drill, for gym, for weapon-training, back to drill—and so on and so on. If you were ever late, or had so much as a bootlace broken or undone, the Platoon Commander would just say 'Puttee' or 'Pack Parade'—and it meant one more change back into khaki after Mess that night. Drilled by the Orderly Sergeant, another Cadet, you marched, doubled along the corridors, up the stairs, out of doors, always at the double for fifteen minutes, interspersed with breathers while you grounded your rifle and did press-ups. If the culprit stopped unlawfully, there was a yell and probably another minute added on.

And so the days went by, digging trenches, boxing, bayonet-fighting, drill, fencing, and our academic studies in Law, Strategy, Tactics and Military History. I loved it all, and returned home at the end of the first term, having been placed fourth. Of course it wasn't all work: I didn't hunt because I couldn't afford it, but had endless pleasure running, did well at Rugger and represented the College at sabre. During the holidays I went on riding and learning to play polo.

At about this time came strikes, and I was enrolled as a Special Constable. Issued with a whistle, truncheon and warrant to arrest those intent on misdeeds, I felt very important. I might add *very* important—until such time as I was sent on my beat through a rather unpleasant part of Rugby; my blue and white arm-band was then carefully concealed in my mackintosh pocket.

The second term at Sandhurst ended, and we were told unexpectedly that we'd do only one more—which meant we'd get our commissions six months early. Meanwhile, at the finish of this second term, Arthur James and I were made Junior Under-Officers, the only two out of one hundred and thirty. I'd passed my examinations third and was given a Cadet Scholarship of £110 p.a. Soon afterwards I bought the inevitable first motor-bicycle, an Omega, memorable for taking me in all weathers to my first love, Dorothea Staveley-Hill. My mother was anxious and disapproved (not of the bike), so when the time came for my first Hunt Ball I was not allowed to take Dorothea Staveley-Hill—that would have been too easy—it had to be an older cousin, Angela Gold, who, once there, was surrounded by her boy-friends, and Mike Ansell was of no interest to her or anyone else. I sat in the gallery at the Northampton Town Hall, pretended to doze, and hated the whole thing. Next day when Angela departed, I quietly enjoyed my mother's wrath about 'modern girls', for under the glass-topped dressing-table was a mass of powder. I well remember my mother's voice: 'How very grubby.'

In the summer of 1923 I finished well at Sandhurst, winning the Saddle of Honour for my term; it surprised everyone, particularly those who hunted and kept horses there. I did ordinary things because I couldn't afford otherwise, but I'm glad I did. I'd had the opportunity to lead and command, which wasn't easy, for the platoon was very mixed; there were strong personalities, those who believed it 'not done' to work—in particular some of the Etonian element, although they always backed one at the crucial moment. So, ending my time on a high note, I now felt my mother's responsibility for my upbringing could come to rest. It hadn't been easy, there wasn't much money, and on many occasions she must have thought of my father and longed for his help. It was now up to me. In later years I realised what a task she had been set when my father was killed, and how wonderful she had been.

All my life I'd known that if and when I joined the Army, my regiment would be the Inniskillings. In 1922 they were amalgamated with the 5th

Dragoon Guards (my father's Command) so that made my choice doubly sure. The War Office had said that the two regiments might be reformed again later, to soften the blow; consequently they never settled down together. When I was sent a list of uniform, it was made quite clear that I was to wear the Inniskilling uniform.

During the three months awaiting my embarkation to India I was much helped by my godfather, Neil Haig. A remarkable character, weighing seventeen stone, he'd not married until very late, and then to a charming but very tiny woman. Every other afternoon he caught the local train to Brighton where he played real tennis: it was an exciting performance, for he didn't leave the house until he heard the train hoot, coming into the station; he then ran slowly down the village waving to the engine driver to wait.

The ordering of uniform was a thrilling and extremely expensive affair: two khaki tunics, scarlet mess kit, three drill tunics from Jones, Chalk & Dawson; from Huntsman, three pairs of uniform breeches, three of white for polo; a cloak, two pairs of overalls from Tautz, three pairs of boots from Maxwell's. A special room was put aside at home where polo helmets, boots and gold belt were all laid. When no one was about, like any bride I used to examine my trousseau.

My mother allowed me £200 a year when I joined. Translated, that may seem a vast amount, but our pay was very small, twelve or fourteen pounds a month, and we were expected to do a lot with it. At last the day arrived, and breeched, booted, belted and spurred, I stepped into a first-class carriage at Rugby en route for Southampton and—India. Who would have guessed that almost exactly a quarter of a century later, the kind of life I was about to begin then, and the Raj itself, would have disappeared for ever?

In those days, if I remember correctly, we were allowed one 'home' leave in six years, but few young officers had the money to pay for the journey: regiments were often abroad for as long as twelve years. It was a moving scene then as a troopship pulled out; the streamers could not hold us, nor the band playing 'Auld Lang Syne'. That voyage was uneventful, with no opportunity to go ashore till we reached Port Said, but before we could do so the ship had to recoal, a sight I'll never forget. Up each of two gangways came an unbroken stream of hundreds of Egyptian coolies, all carrying a quarter of a hundredweight of coal in a basket, every man stripped to the loincloth a link in the human chain which, instead of creaking, emitted a steady chant. It must have taken eight hours or more. During all this, young boys risking the danger of sharks came alongside to dive for pennies; when no Regimental Police were watching, they swarmed up the side to perform startling dives from the highest points. It was incredible how they seldom failed to retrieve the many pennies. Boats wove between them carrying Turkish delight, odd bits of jewellery, silks, even carpets. Often the purchasers weren't satisfied, and I well remember one particular case when the soldiers got hold of the mast and tied it to the ship; the 'Gypies' started slinging lumps of coal, returned with interest, until two or three launches appeared carrying the smart Egyptian police in their red tarbooshes and white uniforms.

The slow throbbing down the Suez Canal is something one never forgets: at night the great searchlights bisecting the barren shore, and far into the desert on either side; then the Red Sea, heat ever increasing, rarely a breath of wind, only a flying fish cutting our monotony.

On the twenty-first morning we all rose early to see dawn break the horizon over the white buildings and golden domes of Bombay. A large crowd to meet us, as always in those days of comparatively slow travel. That same evening I left for Bangalore, after we'd handed over our draft.

In India one always had a bearer, in some ways a steward, for he ran the household—and whether you were a second lieutenant or a general, the household was numerous! Henry, a tall Hindu, proved to be quite excellent. He knew everything, and wanted nothing. He paid my syces (grooms) and dressing-boy, he engaged any new servants, looked after my clothes, waited on me in the mess. Once a month he brought his cash book, and it was always correct. His pay was twenty-five rupees a month: about eight shillings a week.

Although Bangalore was in many ways the most perfect station in which to start one's military career, it was isolated; we were the only cavalry regiment, and incidentally the last to be stationed there. The unmarried subalterns lived in a long building about fifty yards from the Mess. Each had a large cool room with a verandah, a dressing-room and bathroom at the back —the bathroom merely consisted of a tin bath and a cold tap, and the bearer used to boil up water in an old kerosene tin. The bed was webbed, for coolness, mine swathed in a green mosquito net. What I looked like in the early morning behind this veil I dread to think. About a hundred yards away we each had our stables, a yard of about ten loose boxes, all gaily painted. So began my career in the most ideal country that has ever existed for the young officer's education as a soldier.

The two regiments within my regiment almost lived apart, not in the case of the junior subalterns but certainly among the more senior officers. We wore different uniform, played football in different colours; and the Colonel did all he could to foster this feeling of separation, which did the regiment much harm, for Colonel Charles Terrot was, to say the least, a very jealous Inniskilling. Fortunately for me, my Troop Sergeant—a huge, scarlet-faced fifteen-stoner, known as 'Hoot' or 'Big Jones'—was typical of the really good sergeant of that time, desperately loyal and determined from the start that

I should never be in trouble. Like many others there, he'd served in my father's squadron at Mhow some fifteen years earlier.

One Captain Bert Buckley kept a pack of hounds he'd imported from England, and twice a week we met in the early hours of the morning to hunt jackal. The country was rough and wild with, every four or five miles or so, a small village of mud huts surrounded by sugar-cane plantations and paddy fields. After he'd gorged in the village, the jackal used to lie up in the sugar-cane, and here we used to draw him, very early, for the dew gave us a good scent. If he hadn't eaten too much the night before, he was a difficult chap to catch in that rough country—few fences other than cactus hedges and very deep ravines. The villagers had never seen hounds before and used to turn out in large numbers, on foot, gibbering with excitement.

Soldiering became tremendous fun, mainly because you had a complete troop: fatigues or duty officers' servants were taken care of by Indian labour, and even the men had a certain amount of help from squadron syces and barrack-room boys, who helped to clean the kit. Thanks to Big Jones, a wrong-doer seldom reached me, let alone the Squadron Leader; Big Jones would give the trooper some extra job or possibly a clout over the ear. In some cases, if he was dirty, say, the men themselves stripped him and scrubbed him with stable brooms in the water trough—everyone was quite happy with these methods, and from that happiness came a very high standard of discipline. You can't have the second without the first. Possibly neither without the other?

I had to drill once again, two hours a day on the square, with another two hours in the Riding School where they explained to me that I knew nothing whatever about riding: back to the beginning, grooming and cleaning my saddlery included, plus one hour a day at the forge learning to shoe, inspected like any trooper by the Squadron Leader.

The Mess was about two miles away and motor-cars weren't very plentiful; an old Ford belonging to the Mess could be hired, and being an Irish regiment we kept a jaunting-car; however we all had our own buggies, very smart, each with our syce decked in our own particular colours—mine wore an orange and blue turban and belt. On arrival, once the horse was removed, the syce was quite content to sleep in the shade until required again.

We played polo three times a week, and I soon had a stable of about eight, at least four of these being troop horses, each with its own syce, who would rarely be expected to look after two. So my 'entourage' must have been ten, including Henry and a dressing-boy—he did little but clean kit and boil the bath water.

Pay being roughly thirteen pounds a month, the Regimental Banker loomed large in most of our lives: a spidery Indian named Girthralli, dubbed 'girthgall'. These Indian bankers were nothing more nor less than moneylenders, only too ready to allow large overdrafts, for they knew perfectly well that one could hardly leave the country until the account had been settled. In some cases, interest on the overdraft exceeded income; consequently many had no home leave throughout their entire service.

Once while convalescing from a rather bad riding accident, I was invited by Captain John Graham, Adjutant of the Regiment, to shoot for a fortnight in Coorg Forest, really beautiful country in Mysore, with every kind of game: buck and spotted deer the most common; sambur, the Indian elk; the barking deer, no bigger than whippets, which barked like dogs; tiger, panther, elephant and bison.

Every day we set off before dawn, each of us in a different direction with his own tracker and *shikari* (gamekeeper), returning about eleven for luncheon, always with something excellent for the pot; three hours sleep through the midday heat, then off once again. We saw a herd of elephant moving across a ride, cut as precaution against forest fire, and I remember being struck by the silence of the forest, even when they were on the move.

On our last full day John and I decided to go together. One of the trackers saw a comb of wild honey high in a tree, which he climbed while we unloaded and sat down. Suddenly he whistled. We quickly reloaded and stood quite still. There, not fifty yards off, stood a very large bison bull. We hardly breathed, then suddenly he scented, looked up and charged. I fired both barrels of my ·500 Express and John followed. The huge bull crashed past us at the gallop less than ten yards away. We knew we'd hit him because of the blood, but there were no signs of his stopping. It's always foolish to follow a wounded animal, so we waited an hour, then traced his path, crawling through thick undergrowth, with long halts, listening, and about half a mile on we found him dead. As it had been my turn to fire first the bison was mine, and in fact all four shots had gone home. He had stood some sixteen hands, weighed well over a ton, and Van Ingen's book of Indian Game shows him to be the third largest bison recorded. And that, to a young subaltern, seemed great good luck.

The apparently deserted forest burst into life, hordes of the natives crowded round to offer congratulations in exchange for hopes of a good meal. By evening all was skinned, cut up and shared, the liver proving excellent but the meat tough and strong tasting. The head I later sent to Van Ingen's to be set up at vast cost—about £25, or two months' pay. When the War came in 1939 I gave it to the Colchester Town Hall, where perhaps it still watches the Mayor and his Corporation eat their oysters.

Towards the end of my first year we received orders to go by road to Madras, on the south-east coast, where there'd been trouble in recent years. Since it was about four hundred miles from Bangalore, we would march in easy stages of eighteen to twenty miles a day, 'showing the flag'. The route lay through country which hadn't been visited by British troops for over half a century, so we were all delighted. Throughout India on the major trunk roads, well-defined camping-sites with water available were kept up, of which eighteen or so had been selected.

Riding at the head of my troop, we set off each day, about six in the early cool, the road through lovely country and well shaded by the banyan tree. Marching by squadrons, troops had about four hundred yards between them in an endeavour to avoid dust—unsuccessfully, and it must have been quite hallucinatory when the phantoms rode into their next camp, white from head to toe. Sergeant Jones used to ride with me, and kept me well entertained; he always carried a lance to pick up any odd bit of saddlery or equipment dropped by troops ahead of us—a nose-bag, water bucket or picketing peg. Being an old soldier, Big Jones never missed an opportunity of 'making' something, and took great pride in it.

In turn, one subaltern and his troop were detailed to act as Baggage Officer and guard, a miserable job, for the mules barely managed three miles an hour unless you made them trot—when the drivers would wail and complain and then there was real trouble. Unless you were always on the watch, these drivers would drop off to sleep on top of their loads, and the mules wander into the sugar-cane upsetting the baggage *en route*. But the country was intensely interesting, for Wellington (the Sepoy general, as Napoleon contemptuously called him) had fought over it, and places like Seringapatam abounded in relics and tombs among the ruined forts.

We marched into Madras as a regiment, mounted band playing, with our Standard and Guidon uncased, and a month's festivity in that city unrolled for us. The Navy was in the harbour, we took part in a tournament, and a Musical Ride, polo, shooting and dances galore. An agreeable way of 'showing the flag', indeed.

The regiment were to return to Bangalore by train, but a couple of us went back early to do a veterinary course at Poona: the course was interesting enough, though its main purpose had been to get Bill Bovill and me there, at the Government's expense, to play polo. Poona, gay and nonchalant as the sound of its name; but I fear we did little in the polo: we weren't good enough, because although joined by Charles Keightley, a good player, our fourth member, Colonel Charles Terrot, was of little use. Nevertheless a great thrill for me, being my first proper tournament.

Soon after, the regiment moved to Risalpur, the cavalry station near Peshawar; from here we could quickly move to the Khyber or Malakand Passes over the now legendary North-West Frontier. It took about a week by train. We found a new and consequently well-laid-out cantonment, with polo ground in the centre, unused until we arrived. Irrigation had recently been brought, so that trees and gardens sprang up most magically, literally almost overnight. More prosaically, water came by canals from the Swat Valley beyond the Malakand Pass, then was distributed in shallow concrete channels throughout the cantonment; on certain days, an engineer opened sluice-gates and our gardeners steered water where required. They were thus able to grow anything.

My old bearer, Henry, had left me (a Hindu being quite useless there) to be replaced by Mohmand, a small Mohammedan who became a truly great and loyal friend. He ran what we can only call my staff: sweeper, dog-boy, *bhisti* to carry water, *mali* to do the smart garden, *chokidar* or night-watchman. The last three I shared with Charles Keightley and Alec Scott, for we lived in the same bungalow; the *chokidar* slept on the verandah, which ensured that we were never burgled. Barracks being about a mile from the Mess, our mode of transport changed to bicycles: quite a feat, pedalling off to duty as orderly officer, to keep one's blessed sword from getting caught up in the wheels, each of which, incidentally, had two tyres, for grass and road were littered with some sort of very prickly seed about a quarter of an inch in diameter.

At times we were sent to demonstrate to the tribesmen what they might expect if they gave trouble. I well remember one occasion: our composite force—a squadron of cavalry, a battery of artillery, a troop of machine-guns and a company of infantry—was detailed to 'destroy a village'! We moved off late one evening and bivouacked for the night in the open. Heads of local tribes were entertained to a tremendous breakfast by the Brigadier. A special village had been built up the valley and we had to destroy it: we attacked, dismounted under cover of machine-gun and artillery fire, tracer bullets leaving little to spectators' imagination, after which Sappers moved in and blew up every house. Then another magnificent feast, and the tribesmen rode home—well, thoughtful, I think there's little doubt.

Pathans are great fighters and sportsmen as everyone knows; many served in the Indian Regiments and then went back to their villages to help train their friends.

As for hunting, our hounds remained at Bangalore, for this country was hardly worth hunting. On my way home one day, a hyena appeared and with my trumpeter I hunted him down at full gallop over very rough country, eventually killing him with my sword. There was a celebrated cemetery for horses, near a place called The Marble Rocks; once destroyed they didn't have to wait long for the vultures, and sometimes passing we would see these, gorged and swollen; we'd chase after them with polo sticks, as they taxied sedately along, to rise gradually into the air like huge aeroplanes. Another image is associated with those vultures: they were not long invisible when, at that time, Parsees hung their own dead near the top of the towers of silence.

In India one either played polo or 'pig-sticked'. No pig-sticking in Banga-lore. At Risalpur, we had the Central India Horse, who could provide at least three good teams, and the Guides at Mardan not far away. So, a wonderful chance to improve. We had four grounds, two of which were flooded each week, and it was an astounding sight as two hundred Indian women on their hunkers gradually worked across, removing weeds and replacing divots. Three days we played, three we practised. At Mardan, the Guides for more than a century had guarded the Malakand Pass; their officers played tra-ditionally in khaki breeches and helmets in case they should suddenly be summoned to ride to defend the Pass. This place was to me pure Henty: twenty miles away the narrow pass, with beyond a fort any of us might have coveted at Gamages, and above that mud fort the Union Jack always floated: the gateway to Afghanistan. And through that pass, as they had done for millennia, camels brought up carpets from Persia and silk from Cathay, to Mardan bazaar, where—coming down to earth—we bought pyjamas after much bargaining.

During those three or four years at Risalpur I really learnt my polo, and much of it from Charles Keightley, who later commanded a corps with great success, and whose fanatical attention to detail, if anything, even exceeded mine; no American football team could have rivalled us as, huddled over match-sticks representing the players, we sat for hours, analysing and planning.

Inevitably, I suppose, I hankered after the chance to shoot a tiger—but this set of reminiscences has a difference: if one had plenty of money it was easy, one merely took a good shoot and hired a crowd of beaters; out of the question for me. I'd been on a rather arduous Signal Course in Poona and had gone down with an attack of jaundice (whether due to buzzer or the hypnotic heliograph I couldn't decide) and, while recovering, determined to apply for leave at the end of the course and try to 'get a tiger'. Having passed out with a number one certificate, which pleased me greatly, Freddie the dachshund, my faithful Mohmand and I took train for Belgaum; then, with a couple of tents and enough tinned food for three weeks, we had a two-day trek to the village we would make our base.

Grant, our *shikari*, welcomed us. A thin half-caste, badly dressed, European fashion, who obviously enjoyed his glass of whisky, the poor chap was doubly unlucky: not only did I drink nothing but beer but had denied myself the weighty luxury of bringing three weeks' supply. Close to a well, and under the inevitable banyan tree, we set up camp, so absorbed that when we looked up the entire village had surrounded us—and many offered the en-chanting garlands of marigolds. All seemed idyllic, until we discovered ants. Ants seethed on the floor of my tent, in Mohmand's tent; wherever you looked cohorts of ants marched. Poor Freddie couldn't eat his dinner as he hopped from one swarming foot to another. The remedy proved to be my canvas bath filled with water, a soap-box in the middle, on which he ate in peace. We stood the bed legs in tins of water and under a mosquito net I wasn't bothered—neither was Freddie, if he exchanged the haven of his island for my bed.

The plan was to go off with the cattle each day to their grazing: a tiger might follow and kill some bullock that strayed. Days passed, nothing happened. This was the hard way. Late one evening, Grant and I sat by the side of the path; I'd just unloaded the ·500 rifle and was about to pour some tea, when he nudged me gently. Twenty feet away, a tiger. He stood, we gazed at each other; the slightest move of my unloaded rifle and I knew he'd be gone. Suddenly he caught our smell—and off. I was so transfixed by the silence and perfection of his movement, I hardly even regretted his departure.

Not to force my luck, we varied things by shooting for 'the pot' and going after sambur and buck in the hills. Then one night Grant woke me, insisting we were sure to get a tiger next day because he'd found the pug marks of one in a deep dry nulla, or river-bed: it clearly used this route daily, so we must be hidden there before dawn. Five or six miles' walk and we reached the place, about fifteen feet deep, a sandy bed some thirty yards across. Carefully hidden in scrub, we sat dozing, to await the first light. I shall never forget the moment that tiger almost glided towards us down the river-bed. I took careful aim and shot—a terrific cloud of smoke from the black powder cartridge—could see nothing, but knew he'd rolled over; smoke cleared and as he bounded up the bank I fired again.

We sat tight for twenty long minutes lest he were wounded and likely to charge, then crawled down into the nullah: fresh blood all right, proof that I'd hit him, and a clear trail led to thick undergrowth.

The tiger was never found. Returning later with a couple of coolies, we sweated and hacked a way through, half a mile in the noontide heat, till at last we stumbled on the spot where he'd rested and staunched his wound. From there, no further trace. Days, we watched the skies, waiting to sight those circling vultures. None came.

From this episode I learnt deeply a most valuable lesson: use nothing but the best. Buy the best hooks, the best gut, the best cartridges. Had I not bought that cheap black powder, I would have been able to get in my second shot. Lord knows, I was hardly downhearted; at a cost of roughly £20 we'd lived for almost four weeks in the jungle, and acquired a treasure of excitement and experience. But the prize eluded me.

3

Soldiering in England

In the spring of 1928 I boarded a ship at Bombay, sad indeed to be leaving India. Looking back, the reader may think that Mike Ansell and his friends did little but shoot and play polo; in fact, though, we trained hard on the North-West Frontier, with always a month each year under canvas. Horsemastership was the aim, and polo hardly hindered that—after all, the Sepoy General, Wellington, found time to hunt the hare with a pack of hounds, in between tying Napoleon's marshals in knots during the Peninsula War.

Polo in England at that time was a rather different affair. Most teams consisted of a rich owner, two good players who could mount themselves, and, one so-called 'Hired Assassin'. Bill Whitbread, later to become Lt-Col Whitbread and Chairman of Whitbread's, invited me to play in his side, Norton Bavant, and helped to mount me. A match then comprised six chukkas, not the present four, so one had to have at least four or five ponies. I often think of the ladies entrance at the Cavalry Club then, compared with today: no smart carpet, no flowers, only a pile of polo sticks, helmets, boots and the odd dog tied up, waiting for some young officer to finish his cold beef before rushing off to Hurlingham. The three Clubs we joined, Hurlingham, Ranelagh, Roehampton, undoubtedly made for glamour, but after India the standard of grounds could not compare.

I'd been selected to attend a ten months' course at the Equitation School, Weedon—a most unattractive place, built by George III for his guards when he expected England to be invaded. Major-General Jakes Harman was the commandant, Colonel Arthur Brooke, chief instructor; an absolutely first-rate staff of instructors, such as Major Charles Allfrey, Captains Jock Campbell and 'Frizz' Fowler, all of whom expectedly proved themselves great soldiers when war came. Very hard work in every branch of equitation and horsemastership, plus shoeing and veterinary lectures, sword and lance drill thrown in. But a wonderful life. Work over, that abiding love, polo, called—in my case to a team known as the Tigers, famous for their yellow silk vests, the striped cat emblazoned on the chest (which vests were carefully issued just before play and immediately collected at the end).

Weedon could not have been a better hunting centre: Monday, the

22

Grafton; Tuesday, North Warwickshire; Wednesday, the Pytchley; Thursday, the Warwickshire; Friday, Pytchley or Grafton; Saturday, Bicester. Always allowed to hunt three or four days a week (it was considered a vital part of our training), we nevertheless on working days rode from 7.00 a.m. till breakfast, and then another long ride before leaving for the meet by car. Strange to think, today, that if the meet then were twenty or so miles away, a special train took our horses. Stranger still that we nearly always dined out afterwards in a white tie and pink coat. Guest nights, when the local Masters dined in the Mess, often ended quite vividly—a visit to the riding-school, a horse or two brought out to invite those ready to jump bareback; or such incidents as carrying the mess table to the canal, a temporary ship for a high-ranking guest in the Navy. Hunt balls a plenty, always on a Friday, didn't necessarily mix well with Saturday morning's early ride on a blanket, no saddle.

My mother had given me a small open 8-h.p. Rover. We'd think those cars uncomfortable now, I suppose, but what a luxury mine seemed even when, black hood up and side curtains flapping, one drove through a fog-swirling frosty night, head hanging out to see the edge of the road. February 1929 saw a bitterly cold spell; hunting stopped, pipes burst, and even the indoor schools froze up. We were all told to go away except for a few kept to look after the men. One of these, a Canadian, used to skate eight miles to Daventry on the main road to collect the men's pay.

In spring the Equitation School held its own point-to-point: heavy-weight 14 stone; light, 12 stone 7 lb, run together over an unseen course of seven miles. I finished second in the heavy-weight on Flying Fish, narrowly defeated by my instructor Jack Elliott, after an exciting race between Fish and a galloping herd of bullocks to reach a fence first—we won. At the finish we were met, as was the custom, by the Pytchley, mounted fresh horses and —a day's hunting.

Naturally, I was keen on point-to-points. At one, the Grafton, about half a mile from home, I was up with the leaders until going downhill on the flat we turned somersault; I picked myself up, to find my poor horse dead and my right collar-bone well smashed. Only two nights in hospital, but when I returned to finish the Course I found myself mostly watching on a shooting-stick: something of an anticlimax after ten wonderful months. I passed out with one of the three Distinguished Certificates awarded that year, which meant I was qualified to instruct at Weedon.

In June 1929, after a couple of months' leave, I returned to the regiment at York to take charge of the Riding School. Undoubtedly the two real jobs then were Adjutant and Equitation Officer. Charles Keightley being Adjutant, we combined once again to influence quite considerably the life and training of the regiment.

York had long been a cavalry station. The old barracks were in the town, trams passed our main entrance, so the men could easily get into the centre, of an evening, to carouse or whatever. Our new C.O., Roger Evans, came from the Blues, so—no nonsense—he quickly set about amalgamating the two prickly halves of the regiment. He achieved a typical English compromise with our uniform: cap badge of the 5th; Inniskillings' collar badges; the 5th's green overalls; and yellow facings of the Inniskillings. But the spirit he unified wonderfully.

Training, perforce individual, for there were no grounds except a small mud-patch behind the barracks, and about two hundred acres of rough land abounding with rabbit holes and half-dug trenches—hardly suitable for cavalry. But very useful for hunting of a sort: my two dachs, Freda and Freddie, had recently had a litter of seven, so the ten of us hunted the rabbit, very successfully too.

The great attraction of York was the hunting proper, and nowadays many shudder or pretend to be shocked that we hunted so much; but I must emphasise that for a cavalry officer it made a superb training—you had to think quickly, study the country, look after your horse—and while I was away, a younger or non-commissioned officer would be only too happy doing my job, and learning thereby. Charles Keightley hunted almost as much as I did, and I don't think it an accident that, during the war, the 'hunting' Inniskillings had more commands than any other British regiment—that is, they took over at least eight different regiments.

Every day brought an adventure, often amusing, as when, running along-side the railway, Charles took a tumble and lost his horse; an accommodating driver of a goods train stopped, picked him up and slowly brought him alongside the hounds. It was a great sight, Charles on that goods train. And one day, Mud Foster of the 11th Hussars and I, each trying to down the other, got so far ahead of hounds we had to hide in a barn—and hope that when the field went by they'd think we'd just been spending a penny. I don't know if I can convey the special kind of excitement on such a day as when, in a wild part of Yorkshire, the rest of the field left behind, I was alone with hounds and over five miles the 'cry' rose to a sky black with a storm coming up, as on and on we went. Never could I forget that hunt. And when we'd marked to ground, and some ten minutes later Colonel 'Peach' Borwick, Master of the Middleton, arrived, he was, as always, so very pleased that a soldier had been in at the end.

But all this combined with my job, training the recruits and the young remounts; in summer and early autumn, I rode from 6.30 a.m. till late in the evening. Throughout the winter, I was in the Riding School by seven.

At the end of 1930 we moved to Aldershot, where life, or should I say soldiering, began in earnest. York had been a wonderful rest cure, an interim for settling down after India: now we really had to compete. The 7th Hussars and the Carabiniers were with us in the Brigade. For the officer, on the big day when we competed at mounted combat, there were three events: Dummy Thrusting; Sword, Lance and Revolver; and Show-Jumping. Those who succeeded in the Command qualified for the Royal Tournament finals. That first year I came second in all three competitions, which elicited from Ralph Younger of the 7th Hussars—with a smile—'Bad luck, Mike, you're obviously second in everything.' I was very angry and made sure I won the lot on Leopard the following year.

In addition to taking rides and teaching the regimental instructors, I trained our 'Trick Ride'—of which more later. Those involved were so enthusiastic they used to give up their evenings, sometimes missing supper, not finishing till after ten o'clock.

All my army life I enjoyed manœuvres, took them seriously and tried to win. Consequently, those under me, too, were never bored. For one exercise, inspected by General Harman, the aim was to capture some treasure on the other side of the Basingstoke Canal, held by the 7th Hussars and Carabiniers. I had been warned to lead an officers' patrol. Sergeant-Major Gough and I spent all Sunday in a punt, prodding the bottom of that canal until we knew the depth for a very long way. On Monday we swept over unseen, reaching the treasure while our opponents watched behind machine-guns at all the recognised crossings. The Inspector-General liked that. On another occasion, near Brighton, I took out a patrol at night to harass a rather bored Infantry Brigade: in the morning I had to apologise to an irate Brigadier for having let his tent down on him and another officer had to send a box of chocolates to soothe some neighbouring Girl Guides—he'd let down their tents, mistaking them for the Brigadier's staff's. The Divisional Commander, then Sir Archibald Wavell, was delighted we'd been 'successful on all counts'. I got to know Wavell well, and found him a great man, full to overflowing with imagination and enthusiasm.

From about this time until the war came, the Inniskillings were undoubtedly outstanding—we did extremely well in all sports, including football and hockey—and the standard of our young officers was proved after 1939.

Charles Keightley gave up being Adjutant in 1932, when I took over in addition to still being responsible for the Riding School; as Senior Subaltern this meant automatic promotion to Captain at the age of twenty-seven—very young in those days. My day followed a relentless routine: six-thirty in the Riding School; a hurried breakfast and to the Orderly Room; back to Riding School until eleven, then return to the office till luncheon; during the afternoon I either attended the recruits' drill on the square or rode; evening, back to that office. Somehow I still maintained the other interests: polo, show-jumping, hunting and running the Trick Ride. A wonderful life, but quite hard work.

4

Horses

The two main jobs at the Riding School were, first, training the recruits to ride, obviously, which took six months or more, and schooling the young horses known as remounts, which took anything up to a year, depending on the horse. 'Remount riders' were the pick of the regiment. I had about a dozen of them; a much-sought-after duty, though it entailed hard work and long hours. I cannot remember exactly, but something over sixty horses and fifty recruits had to be trained each year. In addition there were rides and instruction for all officers and a few of the Warrant Officers, particularly the more portly Quartermaster-Sergeants, who seldom rode as they were too busy attending to our feeding. We were in the School from seven or eight till five in the evening, for besides training there were fences to be made, and packed uncomfortably with prickly gorse, the ground to be watered and raked, and dummies stuffed for sword and lance instruction.

In order to boost recruiting, most cavalry regiments organised this Musical or Trick Ride. It was performed at the various agricultural shows, which paid a fee, and that went into regimental funds to buy what would then be considered luxuries such as gramophones for the men's messes, or towards our supporters' costs, travelling to Edinburgh, say, when the team played football against the Scots Greys. So, although they weren't paid, the team welcomed a change from routine—not to speak of the possibility of finding a new girl-friend. When I took over the School they already had a first-class Musical Ride, designed by Colonel 'Pudding' Williams when he was Equitation Officer under my father. It entailed much jumping, in one spectacular sequence on and off a bank with machine-guns firing as they jumped without hesitation.

I've often been asked whether I enjoyed polo more than hunting, and which was the best horse I ever had. The answer to the first question's easy: after a good polo match, when I'd played fairly well, I wondered, 'Why the hell don't I school my ponies all winter and not hunt?' and conversely, after a wonderful hunt, 'Why do I spend much-needed money on polo ponies?'

The answer to the second question's more difficult: in the polo world I might perhaps say an Argentine pony called Warrior, rightly named, for at any critical time, when changing ponies, poor Warrior had to come out for a second or even a third chukka. Or perhaps Gay Girl, a grey mare, and equally brilliant. In show-jumping there are two who will always be at the head of the list. Cully Naxter was a very large, rather common horse with a Roman nose: he'd just got to his best, and I think of him particularly on a day when I had to 'jump off' in the King's Cup at the International Horse Show; tragically, he landed on a very wide spread fence, breaking a small bone in his hock, but he nevertheless went on to finish with only that one mistake. I then had to hurry off to play in the semi-final of the Champion Cup at Hurlingham, which had been put back to 5.00 p.m. to help me. We

Mike on GAY Girl..

won that round, and although Cully Naxter and I had failed in the King George Cup I'll never forget his finishing without a fault after the injury.

A troop horse, Teddy, was possibly the best show-jumper I had: never unplaced at Nice in 1939, and jumping two clear rounds in the Nations Cup. But when War came and Teddy went to Palestine with the Yorkshire Hussars, while I went to France in a rather useless light tank, I was glad of this. War is no place for horses.

However, without question, the most unique horse was Leopard, a chestnut spotted grey and black, bought by our veterinary surgeon at York, Adam Hodgkins, who 'saw him trekking behind a tinker's cart looking awful!' Bought him for £20. So this miserable-looking horse paraded on the square with a couple of dozen others: it was customary for the Sergeant-Major's

27

advice to be taken into account, and he naturally preferred a horse that was easy to feed, that would look well. But I took no chances, and begged my Squadron Leader 'How' Wiley to make the dejected chestnut first pick, which he did, saying 'you take him and keep him in your stable'.

Leopard was the most extraordinary horse, standing 16·2, almost perfect in conformation, and although he took time to build up he proved easy to train and would do anything asked. A supreme hunter, he won many hunter trials and point-to-points. Superb on parade, so very proud, and in the Trick Ride he would do anything without a bridle. I could go for a hack or take a ride of recruits bridleless, and yet the next day in some race over fences in a snaffle bit he would take a real hold.

Three years in succession he won me the bronze medal, at the Royal Military Tournament, both at 'Dummy Thrusting' and 'All Arms'—when the rider uses sword, lance and revolver.

He won show-jumping, and on one particular occasion I had to 'jump off' against Lady Wright, who was surprised to see me come into the ring without a bridle, and equally surprised when Leopard won and accepted his rosette lying down. He won without a bridle because he jumped the better if I couldn't interfere with him.

Once in 1934 I had to make a major decision. The King with Queen Mary and the Princess Royal were coming to review the troops at Aldershot, and His Majesty had expressed a wish to see a display of our Trick Ride horses. This would be on a Wednesday and unfortunately I'd entered Leopard for a race at Hawthorne Hill the Saturday before. Dare I risk that when I'd be jumping such things as swords, without a bridle, a few days later? I took the chance because I thought I could win at Hawthorne Hill and had complete confidence in Leopard. And I should have won that race—it was my own fault that I was second—but on Wednesday I left it to Leopard, without a bridle, and there were no mistakes then.

In February 1935 at Colchester, I was giving Leopard a canter before going to Tweeseldown to race, when he suddenly dropped and died instantly from a clot of blood near the heart. I removed the saddle, and wept. Not only a great horse, but human in his friendship, and he was only ten years old.

When I married in 1936 I had some sixty silver cups melted down, and these were made into a model of that superb horse; and so Leopard stands permanently on my dining-room table.

5

Trick Ride

The Musical Ride was a relatively large-scale affair, using thirty-two troopers, and in addition many cavalry regiments produced the smaller display, the Trick Ride. This was cheaper for the agricultural shows, not so large a 'cast' and dispensed with the Regimental Band. In fact the term now seems to me a complete misnomer, applicable for the first year perhaps, in my case, but thereafter the show developed into an exhibition of 'high' training. For example, when members of the Cadre Noir visited us they could hardly believe some of the things Leopard would do. I've always disliked the idea of being an amateur in production, and positively glow with pleasure if someone says, 'Of course, Mike Ansell is a professional at organising a show.' It doesn't mean one receives great payments, or even any payment at all, but I hope it does mean one is efficient.

I quickly realised what fun we all could have if we *really* trained our horses, and not only them but everyone concerned, including the arena party, those with the unenviable task of putting out the props and often standing in as 'live' props—being jumped over, etc. By the end of the first year we'd worked up great enthusiasm and every man in the regiment longed to be part of the enterprise. Mine was a comparatively easy task, for with my intense desire to succeed I could persuade them—and I had the 'artistes' laid on, so to speak—to give up much time in our quest for perfection. Training and much of the practice had to be done late in the day, and if we missed our evening meal and made do with a sandwich and a bottle of beer no one minded.

Pegging occupied most of the first part: very fast, taking up a peg about three inches wide with either sword or lance. Comparatively easy if one had a horse which galloped on a straight line. And this we interspersed with vaulting, which again necessitated a horse that would gallop absolutely straight. The second part was given over to a demonstration of training I don't believe has ever been surpassed.

S. S. M. Gough, Sergeants Lee and Hodgson were magnificent horsemen: Gough, the only British soldier to win the All-India Tent Pegging, a great sport in the Indian Army; Hodgson, the Champion Man at Arms of the

Army in about 1935. I made up the fourth, and thanks to polo soon found taking pegs easier than hitting a moving ball. The outstanding vaulter was a Farrier-Sergeant, Rushton, who could fly from one end to the other (about 120 yards) without landing on the horse: he just vaulted straight over, touching for a split second one side then back again to the other. Not surprisingly, he was our regimental goal-keeper, and the Inniskillings regularly won the Cavalry Cup, and became the first cavalry regiment to win the Army Cup. Of the three or four other vaulters, though perhaps not as agile as Rushton, Lance-Corporal Almond, with his blond wig, tights and a 'mini' skirt always drew delighted applause, while Maddocks rode two horses, standing in Cossack fashion. When he had nothing to do he would gallop them, standing astride, across Laffans Plain at Aldershot.

Then there were the clowns—but here again we determined to have no amateur clowning and Bernard Mills, a great friend of mine, allowed them to join his Circus when on tour in the west. They took their leave for this—it could hardly be fobbed off as a 'Course of Instruction'—but they returned having learnt how to make up, how to raise their hair on end and even equipped with the apparatus required to spin the complete scalp round.

Each year we all had an outing at Bertram Mills' Circus, and once I remember an attractive lady, armed with a long whip, coming into the ring with a mule. Anyone could win a fiver if he or she remained on that animal for a specified time. Usually two or three hired accomplices would come forward, soon to be thrown, but not on the night the 'Inniskilling Ride' was having a busman's holiday. Quickly the word buzzed round, 'Come along, sir. It's a fiver!' The beautiful lady and her act seemed a little surprised to see six new faces eager to win a fiver. I was fortunately last in line, and realised the main problem was getting on the mule—encouraged by the whip, he repulsed any advances with a severe kick. Each had either failed to get on or been unseated when the brute lowered his head and did a fast pirouette. But he was tiring of the Inniskillings' attentions when I got to him. He kicked and I hung on to his leg so that he couldn't move until I'd scrambled aboard; the pirouetting then started but, having long legs, I stayed on. When I got back to my seat a smart page-boy arrived with a new five-pound note on a salver. These didn't readily come my way, and between us we soon spent it.

Human clowns were a must, but we also had a horse clown, the regimental drum-horse, a large piebald standing over seventeen hands, so magnificent on parade carrying the silver drums. He managed to look equally proud pulling a surf-board with Corporal Samuels clinging on, or dressed up as an elephant with a large mask, trunk and bell-bottom trousers.

Pegging had many variations: one might be taken with an invisible string attached—and off would fly Corporal Samuel's skirt or down might come Trooper Daly's trousers. One of the arena party might be hammering in a

peg and as he gave it the last bang it would suddenly whiz between his legs
—and as he raised the mallet in anger that would go too. Gough could peg
with either hand, and sometimes we'd share a horse, I steering and pegging
with my right hand, he behind pegging with his left. Picking up handkerchiefs
or anything else from the ground appeared easy: both legs over to the near
or left side of the horse, one in a strap attached to the girth, and then it was
easy to fall back on the off or right side—easy, that is, until the strap
occasionally slipped or broke.

Jerry the drum-horse couldn't be allowed to remain a lonely comedian,
so we added three small ponies, the first of which, Donald the Shetland, I
bought for five pounds and fetched home in the dicky seat of my very old
Sunbeam. Clipped and with a pulled tail, he certainly didn't look a Shetland.
These ponies came into the arena in trunks or a miniature horse-box, and
would jump, lie or sit down.

Vaulting and pegging were the aperitifs; the second part of the programme
was mainly devoted to jumping. Gough on a big bay mare, Gertie; Lee on
a common bay with an equally common name, Greasy; Hodgson on a
thoroughbred Chestnut, Red Lady; fourth, and the leader, as he deserved,
my Leopard. People have often said, 'Why don't you get someone to put
up a ride such as yours *now*?' They forget that we trained for five years and
had the pick of some four hundred regimental horses. Such conditions no
longer exist, and it would take a very benevolent millionaire indeed to produce anything comparable.

Though I say it myself, some of the jumping was superb. They would
jump anything. As a section of the arena party came running towards and
round us, playing 'Nuts in May', we jumped between them, then other
long-suffering members with sandwich-boards would suddenly duck down
inside while we jumped over them. Trooper Knott drove Jerry dragging a
dray on which were mats; the four of us jumped aboard while the band
struck up 'Thanks for the Buggy Ride, I've had a Wonderful Time'. Occasionally Trooper Knott didn't have complete control of Jerry and moved
off too soon, till one day Knott received a cutting reminder from Gough's
whip. It didn't happen again—and no questions were asked in the House.

By 1932 we had such confidence in these four horses that we decided to
do away with bridles and bits. At first, to create the illusion, we'd used a raw-
hide strap or handkerchief with a string that couldn't be seen by the spectators when we ostentatiously threw off our bridles; but after three years we
found we needed nothing at all as they jumped on and off tables, smashing
the crockery; on and off moving or standing wagons, over a moving line of
fences; and of course while Leopard skipped, Gough and Lee standing on
tubs swinging a long heavy rope.

One night, returning from the Royal Tournament, I was thrilled with the idea: 'Why not use trapezes?' After jumping our last fence, we'd each seize a bar leaving the horses to gallop loose from the ring. When we tried it out the next day, the unfortunate Lee was the guinea-pig, with a broom handle hung from the roof. First time was all right but not fast enough, the second time Greasy leapt like a stag and the broom handle broke.

Each year our fences became narrower, further testing the horses' obedience without bridles. The two hardest feats were asking a horse to jump a line of thirty-two walls, 2 ft 6 in. wide by 3 ft 3 in. high, with no stride between; and asking them to jump eight swords in line, again bridleless, one stride between each sword. (A cavalry sword is 3 ft 6 in. long.)

We demonstrated this high standard of training throughout the country and many still remember it. In 1932 we gave our display twice daily for over a fortnight at the International Horse Show. Between performances we rehearsed the 'act' changes, always on our flat feet to rest the horses: a method I've retained to this day. The band took great care to find suitable music. As Corporal Samuels slid among the flowers on his surf-board they played 'Life on the Ocean Wave', and when we jumped on and off a wooden bed where Corporal Samuels and Trooper Daly in their night-shirts pretended to sleep, naturally, it was 'Let's put out the lights and go to sleep'.

On the last night, the four of us having swung off our horses on to the trapeze, the whole Ride formed a ring around twenty to thirty loose horses and sang 'Auld Lang Syne'. We then opened up and let them go loose, bucking and galloping into the outside collecting ring while we formed up to be thanked by the Earl of Lonsdale, who very kindly presented me with a gold watch.

How could I have known in 1932 that I would still have much to do with the *Royal* International Horse Show in 1972? Even less did I realise that this was in fact to be the first occasion on which H.M. Queen Elizabeth would encourage and visit the show. Here is an extract from the *Daily Mail* of 24 June 1932:

Princess's Delight

The eyes of the crowd at the afternoon performance of the International Horse Show at Olympia yesterday were turned frequently towards the Royal Box, for there were the Duke and Duchess of York and sitting at the edge of a chair, in an attitude of rigid attention, was a small pink-clad figure, Princess Elizabeth. During the Riding Display by the 5th Inniskilling Dragoon Guards, Princess Elizabeth leant far over the edge of the box intent on every move and laughed delightedly at the antics of the three tiny ponies who formed part of the display.

6

America, Ireland, Saumur

During the spring of 1931 I'd badly damaged my right hand (while dummy thrusting, of all idiotic things), and found it virtually impossible to play polo; so I sold the ponies and decided to have a go at show-jumping. It also gave me a chance to recoup: polo being very costly, my pass sheet getting a longer and longer red face. That summer I had my first win, at the International Horse Show, Olympia. Looking back, how fascinating Olympia was! The gay dresses, the flowers and the Gold Chairs: if you were anything in the horse world, you considered it undignified to pay for a seat, so when competing you sat in the Gold Chairs—with your girl-friends, if you wished.

There I first met Paul Rodzianko, whom I consider the greatest instructor of this century. Always ready to help a young officer, he took charge of me and determined that I should win on one of my two horses, Mousie. Early one morning, Mousie found herself at the Duke of York's Riding School, Sloane Square. A large fence had been erected with various unpleasant additions underneath the top pole. Mousie was a real refuser, but Paul assured me he would soon stop that. Confronted by a bewildering wall of umbrellas, coloured rugs and white sheets, Mousie inevitably stopped, only to be severely surprised by a long whip below her hocks, not once but several times as I held her to the fence. She first learnt to recognise Paul's voice of authority. The fence was then lowered to about three feet, and she sailed over to rousing encouragement, with a reward of sugar when halted. Paul said, 'WONDERFUL. You will win tonight.'

'Tonight' I competed in the major Scurry competition of the week; first prize a cup and forty pounds. Almost invariably—whether it be show-jumping, an important polo match or even making a speech—I am terrified: so it can be imagined what I felt that night. Paul awaited us in the collecting ring, and there was no doubt Mousie remembered his voice. A comparatively simple right-handed course, about ten fences, speed the only thing that really mattered. Mousie heard Paul's last few words of encouragement and as the doors opened I started at full gallop. Around we went absolutely flat out,

33

never touched a fence. I knew we'd won, and won with ease. So now I was a Show-Jumper—or thought I might be.

That August, Roger Evans told me that I'd been selected to go to America and Canada with the British Team: Bede Cameron, Chief Instructor at Weedon; Jack Talbot-Ponsonby, 7th Hussars; Bobbie How, 8th Hussars; and myself. We were due to leave in October. Still busy touring the Trick Ride, on the last night at Belle Vue, Manchester, my girth slipped when tent pegging and I had a real stinker of a fall. Apparently I got up and ran to the end of the arena, so well concussed that I mounted Sergeant-Major Gough's jumping horse and continued my pegging. The next thing I knew I was back at the hotel, not too bad, but really shaken up. When I returned to Weedon next morning, Bede Cameron took one look and told me to go home to bed. Needless to say, I only thought of getting on that boat for America the following week. We had an easy trip, and each morning I got fit on a mechanical horse which shook the guts out of one: more usually patronised by liverish old businessmen, though admittedly they set it a notch lower.

No British team had ever been to the U.S.A. before, and a great fuss was made of us when we landed at Boston. The American instinct for publicity being hardly less an obsession then than it is now, the visiting rivals from Canada, Ireland, France, plus the home team and ourselves of course, were shuttled from one entertainment to another during the week's preparation before the show opened—and each jamboree was a background for publicity. For instance, the Drag Hunt luncheon, after which we enjoyed a hunt with the 'drag'. Bede Cameron had been a little diffident about accepting this invitation, fearful that one of us might get damaged before the long tour even began, but there was no refusing.

So we set off smartly dressed in blue uniform—civilian clothes would have been useless to the Press—and *en route* stopped at Lexington to drink a glass of sherry and be shown the spot where the first redcoats were fired upon—the bullet marks reverently pointed out, of course. Thence to an excellent luncheon and afterwards the rather fantastic meet. I remember the young lady riders not so much for their obvious attractions as for the ornate saddlery accoutrements and 'stocks' or hunting ties: how they never cut their chins I couldn't imagine—in fact, some did. Endless photographs, and we were off, i.e. to the start of the line. Hounds led the way, but hardly mattered—soon in full cry after a rabbit or anything else they found. Our Master seemed quite unmoved, the reason quickly apparent: on arrival, we saw the flags providing a guide for photographers and spectators—a perfect 'point-to-point' course, in fact, arranged near a main road. All lined up, and certainly a few hounds joined us, horn sounded and our friends politely said, 'Let the foreigners go first.' I must say I was all for this, having a superb horse, and the hunt soon developed or deteriorated into a race between Dan Corry of the Irish team and myself.

Next, a challenge to polo from the U.S. Army quartered in the Boston District: eagerly accepted, for we all know how Americans love winning and longed to disappoint them. They agreed to mount us as we could hardly be expected to play polo on our jumpers. Poor Bede Cameron, a serious person, had already been shaken by the so-called hunt and was even more shattered by this. He needn't have worried. To the astonishment of a large crowd assembled that Sunday, a gala occasion, we won. A real triumph and, my goodness, were we pleased.

At last the show started, and for three weeks we settled to a quite strenuous routine, one of the most exacting parts being the daily 'fork' luncheon, when we stood about trying to be sociable while invariably answering the same questions: yes, the horses *had* had a good journey; yes, we *did* enjoy being in America; and yes, we *would* hope to do better in the near future. The evening performance seldom ended before midnight, and we were then expected to go on to some party, so we soon had to divide these labours—one pair for the luncheon, the other for the evening session. The whole thing was similar to Olympia. Attendances were good, and lovely ladies tried to blind us with their jewellery displays. Socially we could hardly avoid being popular—we all had smart uniforms, didn't look too bad, and anyway the reputation of the British Cavalry Officer stood high. Even my green overalls were admired. But our equestrian successes were not so much admired.

The first three or four days of the show nearly brought us to despair, the courses more difficult than anything we'd experienced in England. For example, we'd never expected to find a course starting with a treble. Local papers revelled in our failure, their cartoonists sketched our horses surrounded by flying bars with such captions as: 'Gee, what a half-back So-and-so would make. He'd go through anything.' Rather demoralising, and we felt the show authorities had begun to wonder why they'd paid our expenses. At last we won, in a competition for teams of three, and that did the trick. Next day, Jack Talbot-Ponsonby won the Grand Prix and the following night we took the Nations Cup. I shall never forget the parade. Each team had to be led by a soldier in his national uniform, but our grooms were busy with the horses and had no uniform; so our hosts provided us with an American, suitably dressed, as they thought, in a kilt and steel helmet. I think it must have been taken from a cartoon of the 1914 War. We also had the extreme satisfaction of admitting to the Press that we'd known all along we were certain to win and had merely been biding our time.

Gangsters were at their zenith just then, with shooting in the streets a common affair. The majority of the police were Irish, and only too ready to draw a gun. Returning to the hotel late one night, we'd just got inside when a car flew past, followed by another, siren howling, two police hanging on the side and blazing away. Just like the cinema. A few passers-by crouched against the walls and presumably hoped for the best. On another occasion Fred Ahearn, of the Irish contingent, was coming home on the subway when two men got in supporting a third. At the next stop the carriage emptied save for these three, Fred and his team-mate; and then they realised that the figure propped between the other two was dead—probably being taken out to a suburb to be dumped. Fred and his pal soon left the train too.

From Boston to New York, where we again did well; but the celebrated mad rush of that city I found monotonous. A visit to West Point intrigued us: we were very interested to note the severe discipline, the removal of any individual thought—to such a pitch that cadets had to mark on a notice-board wherever they might be if not in their own small rooms.

Whether it was to the show, to West Point, or to luncheon with the Mayor of New York, always a police escort: over red lights, down streets the wrong way, up pavements to pass private cars, the relentless sirens screaming behind. Publicity, of course, at times very embarrassing: for instance, when a police car raced across a red light and hit some unfortunate young man; he was fined immediately, though it was clearly not his fault, and I cannot believe he blessed British Army Officers as a result.

After all that artificiality, we were glad to come down to earth in more humdrum Toronto, though courses there were unimaginative by present standards: better than in New York, but the aim seemed to be a course quickly erected rather than a good course to jump. I had little personal ground for complaint, however, being much occupied with a very gay, attractive Canadian girl called Marg, whose charms, plus the really excellent hunting, made time pass only too quickly, until we caught the last boat to leave Montreal before the St Lawrence froze for that winter.

All told, we'd done better than expected: Britain didn't specialise then in Show-Jumping, but four good horsemen had proved themselves by winning at polo, a point-to-point they call 'a drag', and the Nations Cup. Such versatility would not now be possible: no British Jumping Team has attempted it and certainly never will.

The following year, 1932, my mother sold her house at Woking and moved to the outskirts of Dublin. I decided to spend my two months' annual leave in Galway, to shoot on the Shannon, and to hunt. Bill Enderby who'd been at Sandhurst with me, now married and Master of the East Galway, lived in part of a large house, Redmount at Eyrecourt, so having stayed with my mother, I motored down in the little Morris Minor, to p.g. with him. Bill was out hunting when I arrived. The owner, Hastings Lambert, greeted me: like many of his ilk, since 'the troubles', he'd seen better times and was trying to make a little ready money out of potatoes or anything else he could persuade to grow on his small farm. Who was I, he enquired, and when told said quite bluntly he disliked all John Bulls. Many an unpromising start ends well, for we became great friends, and he certainly knew everything to be known about stalking and shooting wildfowl. And I've never been slow to learn from anybody.

A large house, very dilapidated; oil lamps and candles; water shy of getting hot—so Veronica, Bill's wife, he and I usually shared the same bath water: under the light of a flickering candle it hardly mattered. I soon became great buddies with a poacher, Mickie Lucas. Like all farm workers, he'd been given five acres and a two-roomed cottage, this one almost on the banks of the Shannon, and although he kept the odd cow, hens and a couple of pigs, he believed it more profitable to leave his hay in stooks, so that when the floods came he had good 'hides' from which to stalk wildfowl.

Those days on the Shannon were idyllic. Everything forgotten, I gave myself up to the bird cries, and listened to the wind. At about four or five in the morning I rose, and Maggie the cook primed me with a cup of tea and packed my lunch; then off to pick up Mickie and we'd drive usually to some cottage near the river, where the good lady had the eternal pot of tea ready. And we'd sit until just before dawn, and then into the punt.

As light came I'd be prone in the front, the long-range four-bore pointing, a twelve-bore ready to hand; Mickie lying on his back, paddle well into the water. A frosty morning with perhaps a little fog. It was as though everything about us were hovering, held in suspension. The paddle made barely a sound as we listened and hardly breathed. Until we would hear a pack of teal or widgeon, and plan our approach. Both still, a pile of reed at the head of the punt, not showing a movement, Mickie would paddle down nearer and nearer. And I waited, straining my senses for the moment to lift my head. Then I did. If our approach had been good I got in my shot; but more often than not they'd be gone and I lowered my gun.

Easy to talk now. I loved it at the time, but if the same thing could happen today, and I could see, I'd take a camera not a gun. And how I wish I could paint. When successful, we moved in quickly to finish off any wounded with the twelve-bore, and went on our way. When day grew up, the temperature rising, it was useless following the river; we'd pull into the side, walk the bogs for the odd snipe, then take our sandwiches to one of those many cottages so generously given by the Irish Government—too soon to become useless, as they slowly sank into the bog.

I often think of those days—their pattern so like fishing, though that came much later—of my return to Redmount, after the evening flight, when I'd lay out the bag on the kitchen floor and watch Maggie's expression.

When Bill could spare a horse, I hunted with his hounds over a wild and very varied country, great hairy unjumpable fences, walls, banks with areas of bog, and sometimes no fences but the Irish (or for that matter Devonshire) kind—a gap plugged by an old iron bedstead. Even in hunting I was competitive, I regret to say—well no, I don't regret, because I believe in it. Many try to convince you that they hunt merely to watch hounds, not jump fences, but I really believe all young horsemen should want 'to have a go'. And then how wonderful are the rare moments when you find yourself alone with hounds; their incredible cry as they stream on. One of the two best hunts of my life took place there: the know-alls were quite sure I couldn't get across what looked to be rough open country but was in fact a well-known bog. But the summer had been dry and I hit lucky with a five-mile point and hounds to myself. Sometimes it pays not to know the country. The mask of that fox is in my room to this day.

I've been lucky and had some superb horses, all of whom would go where asked. Tallulah, a common mare, so called because I bought her one morning after a night out in London—I'd seen Tallulah Bankhead and heard that inimitable voice. Tallulah was one of the few to jump for pleasure the railway level-crossing gates at Weedon Bushes. Perhaps these are selfish pleasures—alone with hounds . . . widgeon, teal, mallard, pintail, the rare goose, spread out for the admiring eyes of Maggie the cook . . . a fine fish hooked . . . a splendid flower grown . . . exultation when our team have won —what does it matter? They are things I want to remember. And an early cold breeze, lying in the punt, waiting for the first duck cries, longing for dawn to break.

I think it must have been the influence of Paul Rodzianko, who by this time was helping me train the horses at Aldershot, or possibly my having made friends with Henri de Breuil in Canada, that decided me to go to Saumur, the French Cavalry School. A natural gravitation, for I'd become desperately anxious to learn more of the higher arts of riding. My father had been there on a short visit in 1912, and was about equally impressed by their horsemanship and despairing of their horsemastership—this latter judgement vindicated by the French Cavalry's sad failure in 1914. So I asked permission to go to Saumur for two months, in lieu of leave; the War Office agreed, and was helpful in all but financial arrangements, and thanks to my so-called fame at polo and with the Trick Ride, I was accepted as an unofficial attachment to the celebrated Cadre Noir. These proud men in their black uniforms emblazoned with gold were not only the world's *élite* in the tradition of horsemanship, but felt themselves to be the *élite* of France.

Doubtful that I've ever worked harder: in the saddle from seven to twelve without a break, then a meal with the few instructors who weren't married —an indifferent meal, for these officers saved every penny for their weekends; afterwards a round of whisky poker to decide who paid for the coffee; then back to our horses till six. The school was magnificent, and to me a church. Before entering, boots were cleaned by a soldier at the door: how could any great horseman hope to ride with dirty boots? Afternoons, I took my horses to a school on my own, trying out various aids, carefully watching the result in large looking-glasses which adorned the walls. Yes, Saumur was the very heaven of riding.

Sundays, I used to hunt with the staghounds in large forests about forty miles away, where members wore the traditional golden brown velvet coats with purple collar and cuffs and, to complete the atmosphere, everyone carried a hunting horn. All around calls were being blown, joyfully signifying they considered it a good hunt, or because they'd sighted the stag, or perhaps they'd got lost and considered it a rotten hunt. The ladies all rode side-saddle and wore the tricorne hat. My first day with Bizard's hounds, we killed, and the stag was taken back to the hunting-lodge for the final ritual. First the members had an enormous luncheon with plenty of wine, then we formed up near the kennels where the head and skin had been propped over the remains—remains only, for any tasty morsel had been removed by the staff or foresters. Members in one line faced the hunt staff in another, and each party in turn blew a call, delightful even to my unmusical ear, after which the hounds ate the residuum. A good lady whispered that I would be given the 'slot', adding, somewhat to my horror, that it was customary to give the huntsman a good tip. How much? I quickly enquired. Three hundred francs, came the unpleasant reply—for as usual I was very short of money and did not in the least want this slot. Back at my hotel, I hung it by a string out of the window, but when the time came to return home I'd forgotten all about it, so the expensive memento, or rather, smell, remained behind.

On the last day, I was shown to the Galerie d'Honneur, for Commandant Lessage had decided the Cadre Noir would perform a 'reprise' in my honour. There I stood, literally on the red carpet, transfixed by that magnificent silence—for it is the silence of their performance which is so unforgettable. At the end a salute, then Lessage came forward, riding Tane, to present me with one of the instructor's whips. I am proud of those black and gold rings. They are seldom given.

Certainly I learnt more about the art of riding in those two months than in all my time at Weedon, *but*, had I not been *there*, I would not have been capable of learning. In that way, I believe I became a balanced horseman. Sometimes I wonder, though, why I didn't spend all my life riding 'High School'—I use this term advisedly, for the word *dressage* is now used far too loosely, much of what passes as such today being really what I call schooling or nagging. At Saumur I learnt the wonderful feeling of being part of a horse, perfectly balanced, so light and obedient. Nothing, as we too often hear, on the bit (which is more usually on the *hand*): these horses were ballet dancers, and Lord Wavell's words, 'He must learn to obey with the proud

39

obedience of the soldier', applied absolutely to them. I went twice more to Saumur and learnt the truth of that saying, 'The more you learn the more you realise how little you know.'

Meanwhile, Europe was changing. About 1933 I accompanied 'Pudding' Williams to Germany. He'd been asked by the Directors of the International Horse Show to go and see a drive by 'trotters' and, if good enough, to invite them to perform at Olympia the following year. We stayed on at the Berlin Show, a good, indoor affair, except that only two teams competed: the Germans and the French. The Germans turned out to be by far the better, yet for diplomatic reasons they wanted the French to win. It was agreed that the teams should exchange horses. The Germans still won. I only mention this show because I had the experience of meeting Hitler there. We didn't think much of it at the time: 'Pudding' and I were being entertained in the Director's Box when the invitation came; someone led us to the 'presence', flanked by Goebbels, and Goering, resplendent in pale blue uniform with yellow facings. Later I met Mussolini at Rome, Franco in Madrid and (though I shouldn't perhaps classify him as a dictator) de Gaulle before the fall of France. So with the exception of Tito I suppose I might say 'Full House'. But I didn't hold them in my hand. And they weren't cards.

7

A Polo Tour

Although I sensed rather than thought about it at the time, 1935 marked the end of something, and the beginning of several ends. It was Silver Jubilee year, and King George V died a few months later, early in 1936. In June 1935 I was appointed an instructor at Weedon, and though I felt pleased and proud, it raised several question marks: like many others, I knew that 'horsed' cavalry was finished, would never again be used in modern warfare—and yet we felt war coming. Undoubtedly the cavalry regiment had been wrong to fight mechanisation. Then, from my personal point of view, I was now playing polo better than ever before and wanted to make the most of it. Spring had been perfection: I'd played at Westonbirt, in Gloucestershire—the aubretia unforgettably glorious against the stone in that part of the country—and pondered these problems as I lay in the sun, holding on to a couple of ponies while they grazed. And wondered why the dandelions seemed to be the best I'd ever seen.

For polo was in fact going down in a blaze of glory. So long as cavalry proper existed, the Army to a certain extent subsidised the game; in a very few years that backbone went and the rich owners were decreased because of war and taxation. I've often been accused of commercialising show-jumping, by which is presumably meant that I've produced the sport so that it could pay its way—I'm delighted to plead guilty. During the 1930s we had the opportunity to make polo a spectator sport, and had we done so there would have been sufficient money to send teams to America, where I'm sure we could have won and thus increased our pull over the crowd. But the England of 1935, which now seems unbelievably remote, was still plagued by rather pathetic social distinctions. For example, Hurlingham being a club, a very *élite* club, the public might watch the games from the Public Stand, an old-fashioned affair looking straight into the sun: on no account were those people allowed to walk across the ground and mix with the members. The changes instigated by John Cowdray in 1948 and later by Prince Philip came, alas, too late, and polo's orb slowly set. An utterly stupid waste, for it is a superb game to watch when top-class.

Hardly had I installed myself at Weedon when I received an invitation from the Hurlingham Selection Committee, to go to America with their team the coming September. Too many fine dishes for one course: a real dilemma. Major Bede Cameron, the Chief Instructor, explained that he couldn't reasonably be expected to give me leave in my first two months. I would have to make up my own mind: to give up the appointment, or give up my place in the Hurlingham team. The challenge of mechanisation, and the worrying thought that it was overdue, in fact, decided me: polo might take me away for a year, but Weedon would take me away for three during the vital stages of the cavalry's change-over to mechanisation.

So, across the Atlantic once again, on the 'American Farmer', our ponies on the foredeck all stabled in small loose boxes, and we even had a space in the middle, covered with peat and sand, for exercise. When calm—and it usually was that voyage—we could ride at a walk and give them endless turning. As 'Chicken' Walford and I sailed into New York, we felt we'd come to conquer. The others soon joined us, having travelled by air, with their wives. It perhaps sounds a bit puritanical but I'm still fairly convinced that this kind of team is better without wives, who are often too eager to jump into discussions and even build up trouble; they're apt to sit around counting the mistakes of other members of the team (i.e. not their own husbands') and become extremely excited if those same husbands are dropped.

During the first week we came up against a team with two exceptional players: one of them, Rube Williams, I'd been primed to mark—to ride him, ride him, and not bother about the ball; which I did. Rube, a very tough customer, didn't like it, and lost his temper. I'm not sure that sort of marking is really good tactics; it's apt to become negative, and, however brilliant, you won't always prevent your opposite number from giving you the slip. Anyway, we won. The following day we stayed at Rumsen, and intended to bathe. I've never been so frightened: each time I attempted to go in, a vast Atlantic wave rolled me back on the beach with a few cuts. Never was a great swimmer, and I didn't enjoy this. Our last match before leaving for Long Island, in the final chukka, I rode into a back-hander from one Perkins; his stick came up and gave me a real crack on the wrist. Although I had to leave the ground and the pain was intense, a local doctor assured me nothing had been broken: merely a bruise.

We moved to Long Island, and here the team split up. A busy time, for apart from playing, the ponies and grooms were my responsibility *and* I had to keep the accounts. The wrist still very painful, I could hardly hold a stick, so the doctor suggested that for the next match I should have an injection, both before and at half-time. Useless. I had practically no strength in my arm. When the injection faded and the pain seemed fairly unbearable I had the wretched thing X-rayed. Sure enough the answer signified a chip off the bone and no more play for a month. Disaster. I can't think of another time when falls or any mishaps have prevented my playing.

The Meadowbrook grounds were unbelievably good, and fortunately I played my only game on the number one pitch: it's only used about a dozen times a year—the Wembley of the polo world. Consequently, tactics changed:

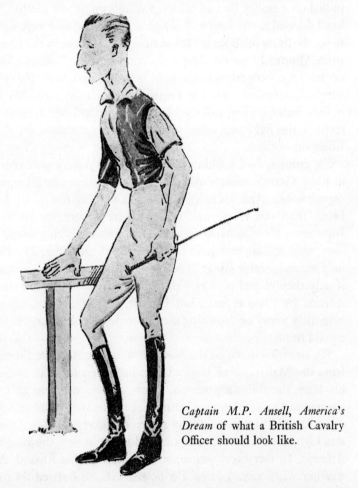

Captain M.P. Ansell, America's Dream of what a British Cavalry Officer should look like.

you could always gallop knowing the ball would come to you in the right place. On bumpy ground a player is always hesitant, ready to hook up and turn on the hocks: much more tiring for the ponies and it slows the game. In America, therefore, a faster game enabled them to use bigger ponies. Also the famous Yankee quantity: at Meadowbrook there were at least eight grounds, at Hurlingham two. On one of the former, after a game, our friends the spectators swarmed over a wire fence protecting the ponies, and for half an hour we sat signing polo balls—a rather difficult object on which to write.

43

It is always interesting to see the best of anything, and during my two visits I was fortunate, for in 1931, when at Boston, we were taken to see Harvard play Texas at American football. Fascinating, for apart from this type of football there was much entertainment between. The two brass bands, that of Harvard having the biggest 'big' drum I have ever seen, pulled on a trolley by two students while two others beat it. And the Texas band dressed as cowboys and cowgirls. In Toronto we were equally fortunate to see the finest of all ice hockey matches: that between the French Canadians from Montreal and the Maple Leaf team from Toronto. On this second occasion we were taken to the fight between Max Baer, the reigning Heavy-weight Champion, and Joe Louis. Louis was superb. No trumpets, but quietly into the ring, followed by the flaunting Baer. Almost within ninety seconds the fight was over, with Baer lying flattened on the canvas, and Louis untouched.

So, grounded—I couldn't play anymore in America—I kept fit swimming in Ebby Gerry's swimming-pool and dancing literally all night to Harlem's superb bands. And, incredibly, we drank nothing but coffee. In a sense I did better than our team, well beaten when we got up against the Guests, Ingleharts, Gerrys, Mills and the like. Just not well enough mounted, too slow, although we may have been as good at the game. The Press murdered us. One memorable sting: 'These Englishmen, their accents are perfect, but if only they played polo as well as they speak.' I suppose one shouldn't be worried by Press reports, but I'm afraid it affects me, either making me extremely angry or drowning me in the depths of misery. If the former, it's a good thing.

We returned home on the *Normandie*, and meanwhile I'd received a cable from the Maharajah of Kashmir: an invitation to go to India and play for his team the following season. Great joy, particularly as I felt I'd been cheated out of my American stint, but the teasing problem was, would I be given leave? Better wait till my return to the regiment, I decided. My heart was high, the *Normandie* did a record trip and flew the Blue Riband of the Atlantic. In fact every *passenger* was given a Blue Riband. At Dieppe the weather was lousy. I knew I'd be sea-sick, so hurried on to the Channel steamer and managed to get a berth in a day cabin: to find myself sharing with that very attractive red-haired actress, Constance Cummings. She certainly was attractive. And I was not sea-sick.

What the weather was like when I reached London I don't know, but I went straight to the Cavalry Club to find a letter from Nawab Kusru Jung (the Maharajah's personal secretary), saying that reservations to India via Venice had been made, tickets were at Claridge's. These reservations were for three days later—and I hadn't yet asked for leave. Having played in London three months, and another two in America, I'd hardly done any soldiering during the past six. Hence a few tremors of anxiety when I took up the telephone to ask for our Colonel, How Wiley, at Colchester. The conversation ran somewhat on these lines:

'Colonel, it's Mike.'

'Oh, Mike, how good to hear from you. Was America fun?'

'Great fun, thank you, Colonel, but I've been asked to go to India to play for Kashmir. Would you mind if I accepted and went to India?'

Pause.

'When do you want to go?'

Pause.

'The day after tomorrow.'

'I think that will be all right, but when will you be back?'

'Well, Colonel, I'm not quite sure, but I think about March.' (That meant six months.)

'Yes, of course that will be all right. Great fun. Don't miss the chance. But I think you'd better come down to Colchester and put your name in the leave book. That would make it easier for the Pay people, otherwise they might want to suggest you go on half pay . . . Can you spare the time?'

'Of course, Colonel.'

So down I went next day, saw all my friends, had luncheon, put my name in the leave book and left for India.

Today this might sound staggering to any young serving officer, but I still believe it right, and were I in the proud position of commanding a regiment, I'd certainly give officers extended leave provided they were doing something worth while. In peace-time, it means someone else will have to do their job, and everyone from the Troop Sergeant must do the next job up—thus preparing them for what will inevitably happen in war, when casualties occur. Of course, good officers will never ask for leave unless they know they can be spared.

Kashmir had certainly arranged everything to perfection, never had I travelled in such luxury. I took ship at Venice and found several old friends on board; also many Italians being sent to the fighting in Abyssinia. Rather a different voyage from my last to India. There is always the problem of keeping fit aboard—in my case *getting* fit, for I'd naturally been unable to play polo for quite a time—so I ran round the deck, did exercises late each afternoon and helped stoke for an hour or two. This last did the trick: stoking in the Red Sea is really hard work. During our passage I received a cable which read as follows: 'Team selected to represent England against America: Ansell, Hughes, Tyrrel-Martin, Guinness. Congratulations, please inform Sanger.' Tony Sanger being on board, it was no easy task to 'inform' him, but he accepted it without demur, we all laughed about it, and in any case the following year our turn came—both Humphrey Guinness and I were dropped.

We landed at Bombay and travelled up to Jammu, which was to be our centre: I stayed in one of the Maharajah's 'guest' houses with General Beauvoir de Lisle, who trained our team. De Lisle was a magnificent person —incidentally the first D.S.O. ever, in 1885—and he had an awkward job welding four very distinct personalities, including Pat Roark, playing at three, handicap ten, and knowing more about polo than possibly anyone in the world. Our conditions were very luxurious and precisely for that reason I took my polo deadly seriously. I'd been provided with the nine best ponies I'd ever had in my life. Each morning I ran for three or four miles, swung clubs for at least twenty minutes, then after breakfast practised on any spare ponies—we never schooled them, that was left to the orderlies. After luncheon, five days a week, we played anything up to ten or twelve chukkas, and in the evening, the General held a post-mortem. (Pat Roark and Tony Sanger hardly listened, but I found I learnt a lot.)

Come the week-end, polo was forgotten and we left for the hills, usually to Serinager, where we shot, or sometimes John Erne and I were sent to the lakes to fish. Very serious fishing: on a lake, watched by indifferent snow-capped mountains, we took it in turn to stand in the bow of the boat with a three-pronged spear. Our mad thrusts at a fish merely pierced glassy water, until, having had enough, we passed the spear to a boatman, who, of course, never failed to get a fish.

The shooting was another matter. One week-end a duck-shoot had been arranged. Seven of us arrived at a lake, seven miles long and three miles wide; we rowed out to a small artificial island, only about twelve feet square, where I found two guns, a thousand cartridges and my luncheon basket. Orders were there in writing: no shot to be fired till 9.00 a.m., the first shot from No. 1 butt; shooting to stop at 1.00 p.m., start again 2.00 p.m., finish at 5.00 p.m.

Each had a counter to hang round his neck; when you hit a bird you were expected to press the button. I pressed regularly, almost every time I shot. The sky thick with every kind of wild fowl—geese, widgeon, mallard, teal, even snipe. Very hot weather, and by luncheon I'd had quite enough. Dead on 1.00 p.m., total silence; our loaders went out to collect the fallen. I opened the basket to find a superb four-course luncheon, with wine, beer and even cigars. Much of it was left untouched, I fear. At 2.00 p.m. exactly, shooting started again, until gradually the geese, widgeon and mallard had disappeared and only teal remained. When at last we finished, I studied the indicator round my neck, surprised to see how many I'd shot and how few had been picked up. Back at the rendezvous lay, or rather towered, a pile 1,360 or thereabouts. Exhausted, shoulder to elbow black with bruising from the gun, head splitting, I longed for the days of two or three brace of duck—not thirteen hundred.

Fortunately, there were more varied week-ends. Once we set off with the Maharajah in shining Rolls-Royces for a shoot in the wooded hills. Near a small village, halt was called, and we changed to mountain ponies. For the first and only time, through the village, I saw a road entirely covered with flowers, lined by all the inhabitants, who threw more flowers in our path and cheered His Highness as he rode past. Next day, each of us stood ready in one of the 'machans', six feet off the ground, which ranged along a cutting through the forest. I had a loader and an assistant, and two guns: one a rifle, the other a twelve bore. What we were to shoot remained a mystery until the last second. Would it be wild pig or jungle fowl? The one sure thing was that I would have the wrong gun in my hand. There would be a wild rushing noise—boar! thought I, grabbing the rifle—and out came a jungle cock.

And so the week-ends passed, but during the week we were well entertained, in more ways than one. The Maharajah, always frightened of being poisoned, had learned to become a quite excellent cook. One day, on arrival for supper at the Palace, we were told we must cook our own meal. Divided into pairs, the guests drew what they were obliged to prepare and settled down before the coke brazier allocated to each couple. In turn a sample was sent to the Maharanee for tasting, and if you failed, you were left to eat nothing but what you'd cooked. My partner John Erne and I were drawn to cook rice, and by some miracle it turned out to be edible. I can't imagine anything worse than being forced to eat nothing but rice.

Personally, I liked the Maharajah. He was bent on helping his people, but had become very suspicious of the 'white man', largely because he'd suffered in a very unsavoury blackmailing affair in Paris known as the case of Mr X, which caused a considerable stir in its day. When we got to Calcutta, for the handicap tournament, I played in a side with the Maharajah. In the practice games, if His Highness played badly, he sulked like a small boy and retired to bed at seven in the evening. Nevertheless, in the final of the handicap, we won. And were only just beaten in the Final of the Open by Jaipur. In those days I thought little of playing eleven or more hard chukkas in a fairish heat. Bombay was much the same, overshadowed by the loss of one of our second team, an Indian Officer, who had a bad fall and died. I naturally remember the funeral clearly, for it was the first time I'd seen a coffin placed on a pyre and we remained there till the whole thing was burnt out.

More cheerfully, Bombay linked me with a most attractive person, Daphne T. We used to dance late into the night at the Taj Mahal, which at that time boasted the only 'air-conditioned' restaurant in India. The T.s also had a lovely shack at Colombo Bay, about fifteen miles out of Bombay—white sand, sea ridiculously blue, shacks made of palm leaves—quite romantic

47

enough, and I certainly made the most of it. However, despite (or because of?) those late nights polo hardly suffered: we revenged our defeat in Calcutta, being the first team for many years to defeat Jaipur, vastly to their surprise. Then, sunset. Just as we were leaving for Delhi, news came through that King George V had died. The Tournament was cancelled, I decided my leave must come to an end, and planned to fly home from Jodhpore. Long-distance flying was a leisurely adventure in 1936; we would come down for luncheon at some airport, and of course we didn't travel at night. I suppose it took about four days to get home.

I had two or three days to fill in, so Hanut and Prithi of the Jaipur team arranged a day's pig-sticking. Never had the opportunity before, in India one usually either played polo *or* pig-sticked, not both. The country was very scrubby, dried up, and although flat had large ravines. The wild pigs, which did much damage to the crops, were driven out into the open where two of us, well mounted, hunted them with a lance or spear. They went at a real gallop, and it was most exciting across this rough country with sudden ravines as hazards. Having stuck the pig there was always the chance he would disappear into thick undergrowth, when we would dismount and follow, on the alert for him to charge.

8

Sunrise 1936

At this time I had an absolute string of horses and ponies. How I maintained those stables at a large house, Berechurch, just outside Colchester, I don't know. Well, the truth is I couldn't, and by the end of 1936, 'statements' had become so red they practically burnt their envelopes: I had to give up polo. But that is to anticipate; this was to be the greatest year of my life, and even my chagrin at being dropped from the English team vanished when I met Victoria Fuller. I was staying at Hyam when playing at Westonbirt, and one evening Trevor Horn told me that Victoria was coming to dine: I sat next to her, but how can I convey exactly what I felt at that first meeting? Her undoubted beauty struck me as it had so many. Did I fall in love at that moment, as story-books say? Possibly not, but the impact was severe. A few days later she came to tea after polo, then we had a dance at the Hare and Hounds Hotel—I managed to sit out with her a good deal: quite a feat, Victoria being constantly sought after—and each day I wanted to see her more and more, until finally I had to admit to that ridiculous 'defeat' known to all lovers: I wanted to be with her all the time. Out of the question. She had her doubts, and soon left for three months in Russia. Polo took me to London, but my thoughts were always with Victoria, and I wrote to her regularly.

Humphrey Guinness, Frizz Fowler, David Dawnay and I now became the opposition for the English or U.S.A. teams, twice a week, and oddly enough we had the best polo ever. In our first match at Ranelagh we almost beat the English team, which gave the Press plenty to write about. One incident during the Champion Cup showed how hotly feelings ran that year. We were playing against the English Captain, Eric Tyrrel-Martin, playing for Texas Rangers, and he unfortunately got caught standing on the ball right in front of the main stand; Humphrey shouted and encouraged Hexie Hughes to ride into him, which he did, whereupon Eric hit Hexie over the head with his stick. Whistles blew, pandemonium, and we were given a penalty—Eric was warned off for the remainder of the Champion Cup—and the hoardings of the evening papers read 'English Captain warned off'. I think it's unique in the history of polo.

Victoria had now returned from Russia and I intensified my siege. I got myself invited to Cottles, but Roland Forrester-Walker, Victoria's stepfather, obviously thought she should marry someone more acceptable than an impecunious young cavalry officer. Then a stay at Exford, in Somerset, Victoria also there, where I hunted and, although I say it myself, made a superb miniature rock garden which won first prize at the Exford Flower Show. My stock began to rise.

After the Champion Cup I rejoined the regiment, and we had a month under canvas on the Sussex Downs. (The regiment's route by road from Colchester to Lewes played havoc with the traffic then: it's amusing to think what might happen now.) Chris Fuller arrived on the scene, for an attachment, since he was a Wiltshire Yeoman. Undoubtedly he'd come to carry out a reconnaissance on me, under orders.

During that month Victoria stayed with some people not far away in Hampshire. They invited me over to play tennis; we *did* play tennis; but somehow when I wasn't playing, Victoria dropped out too. Luckily for me she dropped out once too often, and I finally persuaded her to say Yes. That evening at dinner, I remembered to take only one plum, to make certain it would be THIS YEAR. And sure enough, after the usual engagement ritual, we agreed to be married on November 17, at St Margaret's, Westminster.

When people are in love and mounting to the crest of the wave, everything becomes blurred, and one tends to remember slightly idiotic details. I was staying at the Cavalry Club, and on the wedding morning Hicks the barber cut my hair, then persuaded me that I should be specially shaved for my wedding. Like a fool, I agreed, only to itch like the devil for days afterwards. Humphrey Guinness, the best man, and I arrived at St Margaret's after luncheon at the Berkeley, and I went straight to the choir to give them their 'orders': 'Sing like hell.' Now I conjure up so vividly how wonderful Victoria looked as she came up the aisle—I thank God I had no inkling of the difficulties, worries and even horrors we would have to take on together during the next thirty years.

Before going to Corsica we wisely decided to spend three or four days at Moynes in Essex, at Victoria's sister's house, which she had lent us. There we enjoyed the peace and revelled in reading the accounts of our wedding. On the Saturday I suggested I should introduce Victoria to professional football, which I have always enjoyed. And so on the Saturday off to White Hart Lane to watch Tottenham. *En route* we found ourselves in a queue of cars, and gradually I moved up to the head of the line to find a police car leading the procession. It was doing just under thirty. I trod on the accelerator and shot past. Down I came to thirty, and at the same time heard 'the gong'. We stopped, and I explained that I had only exceeded thirty to pass them. By this time one police officer had produced his notebook, and the other looked at my licence. Then Victoria said, 'Oh please, Officer, we are on our honeymoon.' This did the trick. The notebook was put away, and on we went.

Most of the honeymoon was spent in Corsica, stopping off briefly at Marseilles. There, Victoria decided she didn't like my moustache—so I removed it in the bath. Then she wanted it back. A glorious sunny November morning welcomed us to Ajaccio, and a car took us to Ile Rousse, a tiny village on the northernmost tip of the island; the road twisting through the mountains, till it dropped down to 'our' Hotel Napoleon Bonaparte. We were the only people staying in that vast hotel; most of the furniture was covered in dust sheets. It really didn't matter. Our days were mostly spent in walking, and at times my Victoria was not too keen on that. Then we would take a car to some place, walk up into the mountains, sometimes into the clouds.

There was the earnest taking of photographs, with always some chosen bush or tree in the foreground—to add to our artistic endeavour. The day on the golf course—not a huge success. Lying among the rocks. And, of course, a day's shooting. A local landowner invited us to this last. I asked what we were to shoot. 'Anything,' he said, 'from wild pig to *petits oiseaux*.' Who could refuse such an invitation?

On arrival at his house, he gave me a smart double-barrelled gun, twelve-bore, and a waistcoat as bandolier, which, explained the owner, contained cartridges loaded with No. 2 shot for the wild pig, 4 for duck, 6 for partridges and 12 for the *petits oiseaux*! So, tense with excitement, as the cliché goes, we set off in single file, guns at the ready and loaded for the wild pig. We saw nothing, but approaching a large lake I was instructed to change to No. 4's for the wild duck. Another half-hour's tramp in the hot sun, till my host indicated that I must change to 12's, for the *petits oiseaux*, at the same time explaining he now had to return home.

Victoria and I settled into a boat and set off in pursuit of well-trained coots. Whenever we approached a bird, it quickly dived, to appear a few minutes later out of range. Even Victoria tired of this hilarious hunt, and we pulled for the shore, had luncheon, and she continued to enjoy the sun, while I, for the honour of Great Britain, pursued screeching blackbirds from bush to bush. They were quite as elusive, or well-practised, as brother coot. Late that evening, when we returned and handed in gun and cartridges, I think our host seemed relieved, for there was no need to clean the gun.

We left Ajaccio early one morning. All went well till the time came to land. A number of young French soldiers had accompanied us in the flying-boat, and in spite of the hour they'd enjoyed a large amount of brandy. We landed all right, but had to wait some time for a boat to come and bring us in: the sea very choppy, and poor Victoria whiter and whiter as the minutes passed. Too much for the French soldiery: each in turn seized a bag and was sick. I whispered to the ghost beside me, 'Remember you are British.' And she certainly did.

We saw the New Year in at Rookery Nook, a small cottage we'd taken three or four miles from Colchester: most attractive but *very* small; I had to go down on my hands and knees to get to the bathroom. Through the haze of the happiness of my marriage, I saw that polo had to end and I must sell my ponies; more important, it was time I started to work for the Staff College.

Not a good year to choose.

1 Colonel of the 5th Royal Inniskilling Dragoon Guards, 1957–62.

2 H.M. King George V, accompanied by my father, inspecting the 5th Dragoon Guards. H.R.H. Princess Mary is on the left. Aldershot, June 1913.

3 India 1910. An introduction to 'driving' with my mother and sister Bunny.

4 Setting off in a jaunting-car on a fishing expedition with my father in Ireland, 1911.

5 On my pony Black Prince at a meet of the Kildare hounds, 1912.

6 Winner of 'The Saddle' at Sandhurst, 1923.

7 On joining my regiment, 1924.

8 The file on Michael P. Ansell, alias 'Doggie Mike', after a visit to Boston Police Headquarters at one o'clock in the morning.

Form 1052.

MALE

Name _Michael P. Ansell_

Alias _Doggie Mike_

Photo No._____ Dupl.F.P.No._____ Crim.Record No._____

Ref._____

Prints taken by _Sergt. Taylor_ Date _10-19-31_

Bureau Crim. Invest.

Classified by _____ Tested by _____

F. P. Formula $\frac{13}{7}$

M	U	I	M	X
I	O	I	U	U

Ref. _____ _____

_____ _____

1. RIGHT THUMB	2. RIGHT INDEX	3. RIGHT MIDDLE	4. RIGHT RING	5. RIGHT LITTLE
M	8	I	M	18

6. LEFT THUMB	7. LEFT INDEX	8. LEFT MIDDLE	9. LEFT RING	10. LEFT LITTLE
I	O	I	10	11

FOUR LEFT FINGERS	FOUR RIGHT FINGERS

M.-7-'31.

9 Instructing in 'dummy thrusting'. Sergeant Hodgson, later 'Champion Man at Arms', demonstrates. Aldershot, 1932.

10 Leopard, a horse for all seasons.

11 Leopard jumping without a bridle, 1933.

12 Leopard point-to-pointing, 1934.

13 Resting after a rehearsal of the Trick Ride. Jess and I have a comfortable seat on Leopard (*left*).

14 Leopard and I skipping.

15 On to the trapezes, a highlight of the Trick Ride.

16 We take a lift on the 'dray', with Trooper Knott our driver, 1933.

17 On Warrior, training for International Polo versus U.S.A., 1936.

18 Teddy jumping at Nice in the Nations Cup, 1939, when he won 'Best Individual'.

19 British team in line to meet Signor Mussolini in Rome, 1939.

20 The Lothian and Border Yeomanry. A conference, April 1940.

21 Treysa, 1941. An oddly assorted prisoner-of-war group, with myself second
from left.

22 Pillhead as it is today.

23 With Victoria in the conservatory at Pillhead, 1958.

24 Presentation of the 'Standard' to my regiment by General Sir Charles Keightley, 1961.

25 Planning a show-jumping course with my special magnetic board.

26 21 July 1964. The White City at 7.05 p.m. A crisis with the cloudburst. Could we hold the evening performance? We did.

27 Threepwood, owned, trained and ridden by Nicholas, my son, winning the Grand Military Gold Cup at Sandown, 1964. This is the only occasion since 1938 that the winner has been owner-trained and ridden.

28 Beam, April 1965. Although I was the only person fishing that day I caught these two salmon, 18 lb and 19 lb. No wonder I was happy!

29 Fishing at Beam on the River Torridge. Keith and Paula at the ready.

30 Speaking after receiving the President's Trophy, on behalf of the British Team, from H.R.H. The Prince Philip in 1965.

31 After the Investiture, February 1968, Victoria and I outside the Cavalry Club with the family. *Left to right*: Antony, Sarah and Nicholas.

32 On 2 May 1968 the Editor of *Horse and Hound*, Walter Case, gave a dinner for me to which he invited many of my oldest friends, one of these being the Maharajah of Jaipur.

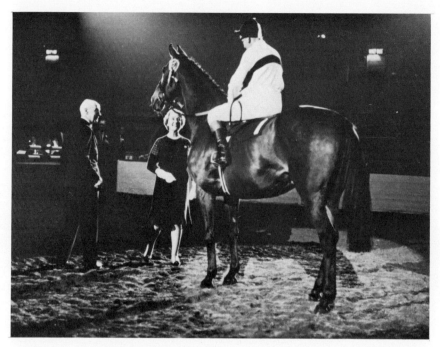

33 Anne, Duchess of Westminster, accompanied by Mr Tom Dreaper, with Arkle and Pat Taaffe at the Horse of the Year Show, 1969. This was Arkle's last appearance in public.

34 A cold morning at the horse inspection before the final of the 1970 Three-Day Event at Badminton.

35 Spring comes to Pillhead. The snowdrop wood.

36 Eileen and I at the Horse and Hound Ball, 1971.

37 The Bog Garden in the making.

38 In my study at Pillhead.

9

Before the Deluge

The last four years of what I will call my old life, 1936–40, were certainly the happiest I have ever known: so happy that I should have been prepared for what the Greeks called *peripeteia*, the sudden dramatic change of fortune. But I only thought of that afterwards. Early in 1937 we knew we would have to find a new house, for with Victoria expecting our first child in August, Rookery Nook would burst its seams. Luck took us to a most lovely place: Wakes Hall, about ten miles from Colchester, looking over a wide valley, a stream at the bottom and plenty of wild duck. There was stabling for about six horses, and a nice little shack for Trooper Peat, my groom, and the two other soldier servants. Mr Percival, the local farmer, had about five hundred acres around us, and for £50 per annum he rented me some excellent shooting, which I shared with four others at a tenner apiece. There were two large woods on our shoot famous for their primroses, and often Victoria and I would lie there among them whenever we had a spare hour. In summer we walked through the valley, up to our waists in meadowsweet, and one day we found a fox's earth—we used to watch the cubs through glasses from the house. On shooting days, Peat and I would ride around and perhaps outside our boundary, driving in any coveys of partridges, until a lorry from the regiment arrived with our beaters, all the men delighted to have a day in the country.

I well remember my first go at the Staff College examination. I really hadn't done much work and regarded it as a trial run, so I didn't do very well and didn't deserve to, particularly as I gave the last paper a virtual miss, leaving after about fifteen minutes (to the astonishment of the other officers) because I was riding a good horse at Cottenham that afternoon. We won comfortably, but perhaps that was not the race I should have won.

In July came the job of commanding a composite squadron on manœuvres in the Hertfordshire area. I had the pick of the young officers and was attached to a Division commanded by General Armitage. Apart from the armoured regiments, each side had one horsed squadron and these manœuvres in fact proved to be the last for 'horsed' cavalry. Although not equipped with anti-tank guns, we soon put that right by going to the

Regimental Tailor and ordering some thirty green flags with a white cross, to represent them; these were quickly produced. If only, in 1939, Hore-Belisha had been able to provide us with real equipment as fast as that Regimental Tailor gave us the symbolic article, the German Army might not subsequently have overrun France at the rate it did.

Among my subalterns I had 'Monkey' Blacker, later to become General Sir Cecil Blacker, Adjutant-General, who even then demonstrated the supreme versatility which enabled him, in 1955 or thereabouts, to box for the Inniskillings (although a Lt-Col), have a picture hung in the Academy, write an article for the *Spectator*, and ride the winner of the Grand Military Gold Cup at Sandown—*all in one month*. Always an enthusiast, on this occasion he set out with my leading troop and during the night we moved the complete horsed squadron seventy-two miles. By early morning we had passed right round the enemy and cut their lines of communication. I received a message from General Armitage full of praise for what a 'horsed' squadron could do, which I particularly cherish *now*, for undoubtedly the initiative and mobility our men showed then served them well later in the Armoured Divisions, where they played an exactly similar role. Much of our success on those manoeuvres was due to 'Monkey' Blacker, who years afterwards told me he had hardly dared stop to read his map: throughout the night he heard the remorseless clippety-clop of his squadron leader (i.e. M.P.A.) and that voice quietly saying, 'For heaven's sake get on!'

At this time manoeuvres were reported in the Press, and of this battle the *Daily Telegraph* wrote:

> The Inniskillings, one of the few horse regiments, put a large body of infantry and the Headquarters of a Field Brigade out of action and captured a Brigadier and Brigade Major. This was an extraordinary 'bag' for a horse cavalry squadron and placed the day's achievements of the 'petrol cavalry' in the shade.

On August 17 my son Nicholas was born in London. I'd been out on a night exercise and coming into the Mess just after breakfast I found my brother officers carefully counting on their fingers, one, two, three, four, five, six, seven, eight, NINE. Nine months to a day!

We'd now been nearly six months at Wakes Hall and were warned that the owners would be returning after Christmas. Again luck was with us, and a little farther from Colchester we found the perfect house in Earls Colne, owned by the sister of General Ironside, later Chief of the Imperial General Staff. Although it was more than I could afford, particularly as we had to pay for a gardener, I went straight to the estate agent to sign an agreement. Returning to barracks, I found a message from the Orderly

Room: 'Please go and see the Colonel immediately.' He told me that although I'd failed the Staff College Exam I must immediately take up a staff appointment as Brigade Major, 5th Cavalry Brigade, stationed at York. So, find another house! And we did, in Malton. The disadvantage of being eighteen miles from my office mattered little, for I had a superb Orderly Room Sergeant, Metherall of the 8th Hussars. This being the proud possessor of two houses is a typical army set up: you take one, and before even getting into it you're moved—and still have to pay, of course.

Our new home, Highfield, lay in the centre of the gallops used by Elsey, a great trainer, and as the Cavalry Brigade stretched from the Northumberland Hussars to the Sherwood Rangers in Nottinghamshire one was in the fortunate 'position' of never being able to be located. Mr Metherall was a great asset running the office, for if a telephone call came from Northern Command, he was only too happy to explain that Captain Ansell was on his way to York: he would then contact me and I would telephone as if from the office, about to jump into a car to visit H.Q. Usually I telephoned from home, for Northern Command had the unfortunate habit of summoning me on a very good hunting day—and sometimes hunting took precedence. Victoria and I were wonderfully happy at Malton; we had many friends, I had endless work, and, needless to say, unlimited hunting.

Meanwhile I worked very hard for my second shot at the Staff College Examination, rising at six each morning to study, even when I'd worked late the night before: I've kept the habit to this day, finding like many others that the mind is clearer at that hour. When the time came, in March, I found all the papers easy—but for one bitter mistake in what was then known as Imperial Military Geography. These S.C.E.s hinged on the matter of time: one had to attempt every question. My downfall read as follows: 'Mussolini has stated that the Mediterranean and the Red Sea is *via* for Great Britain but *vita* for Italy. Is this correct?' Having just had something similar from my crammer, I leaped into the answer; but unfortunately he'd only mentioned the Mediterranean; I did the same—and when I re-read the question, to find I'd only dealt with half of it, I panicked and spent too long trying to correct the mistake. Result, I passed with good marks in every other subject, but the Red Sea scuppered me and I failed in Imperial Military Geography. Had I read that question carefully, or not panicked, my entire future would almost certainly have been different. A grim irony for me now, saying that was the only way in which Mussolini affected my life.

Not long after, I learned that under Hore-Belisha's new regulations, soon to come into force, any officer over thirty-five would be promoted to the rank of Major, but under thirty-five could not be elevated even to fill a vacancy. Luck intervened again, almost as though to console me for the exam fiasco, and I persuaded a brother officer who was leaving to send in his papers a month early—in return for a month's Major's pay. I got promoted just in time, with two or three years in hand: a very good deal.

Major-General Evans now wrote to me what I can only describe on this occasion as a very 'healing' letter:

My dear Mike,

This is a hurried note to say how sorry I am not to see your name in the list of successful candidates at the exam. It is particularly disappointing after your hard work, and I feel for you very much. However, don't despair, Mike! Even if you haven't another chance to take the exam—and I'm not sure about this—I don't think you need worry. A p.s.c. is not everything—*vide* Jakes Harman! Again, there will shortly be a senior staff college at Minley which will be filled by nomination. Primarily the nominations will be from people who have passed the junior college, but special provision will be made for outstanding soldiers who haven't. *I* have no doubt in my own mind that you are outstanding, and that you will be recognised as such wherever you may be soldiering. So I feel that there is no need for you to feel discouraged—there is always room for the really good man. I am not saying this merely to try to comfort you. I feel it to be true, and I owe it to you for all you did for the regiment in my time to say so. And I shall say so to whomever it may concern.

That letter all but dispelled my chagrin; and, indeed, so long as such men are bred, the young need never despair.

Now time seemed to race, through the Munich crisis of 1938, until in the fateful year I received an invitation to represent the country with our team at Nice and Rome in early May. Needless to say, I longed to go, and with some hesitation asked my Brigadier if I could be spared for a month. He was delighted, thank God, and full of congratulations. From early February we trained every Saturday and Sunday at Weedon, until on one of the last weekends, after jumping there, Victoria and I motored to the Aldenham Harriers for me to ride in a point-to-point. I won the race, but felt really lousy with a sore throat. At home the doctor diagnosed quinsy, and the problem was would it burst before we were due to leave. Could I keep it from my friends at Weedon that I was unfit? After gargling an uncountable number of times, feeling desperately ill and sorry for myself, at the very last moment the wretched thing burst.

We spent our first night in France at Fontainebleau, and from there visited the battlefield at Néry where my father had been killed. The same family lived at the farm and they well remembered the English Colonel being brought in to die. The following year, 1940, I had good cause to think of that day: my father who'd died in the first weeks of the Great War, myself near the brink of the Second. But I am still alive.

We slowly motored down to Nice. I say slowly advisedly, because Victoria liked to stop at nearly every French Cathedral, and I fear she wasn't best pleased when I wouldn't stop in Avignon, anxious to be on the spot when my horses arrived.

The Nice Horse Show was different from any other I had been to, the arena dazzlingly decorative and gay with flowers, and an atmosphere of Midi insouciance which made the whole thing seem a festival. Our team, led by Dickie Shepherd of the 7th Hussars, included Boy Butler, a really great horseman, later killed in North Africa, Dick Friedberger, Horse Gunner, and Steve Jenkinson, all of whom distinguished themselves when war came. There were eight or nine teams competing, and the friendliness and sense of comradeship very happy, certainly, because we all felt the impending disaster in our bones. Dan Corry, of the Irish team, a wonderful friend throughout my life, gave me invaluable encouragement and advice as to how to attack the large but superbly made obstacles. When it came to the Nations Cup, we'd never anticipated being in the first three, but my horse Teddy was in splendid form and had already made his mark on the show: he jumped two clear rounds and at the end of the second we were equal first with the French. Although our team was narrowly defeated in the jump off, Teddy received the award for the highest placed horse.

We then motored on to Rome, Victoria loving the country and the people, for she was fluent in French and Italian, and, unlike most of our race, never too proud and afraid to try and speak a language. We stopped the night in Assisi, and walked up to the well of St Francis, which looks so exactly like the scene in those paintings, where birds fly down and gather around him. Rome, of course, a magnificent show: the ladies ravishingly turned out with that something between grandeur and elegance which only they have the secret of, the arena bright with azaleas. Rome still maintains its traditions, and whenever I think of the place I visualise those tall pine trees, like eight or nine witches watching horseman after horseman compete.

Gaiety the order of the day, and we all danced and visited fashionable night-clubs; yet nowhere could we escape that strange feeling, the sense that we were fine friends now but within a matter of months or weeks we'd be on opposite sides, competing not with horses but for our lives.

The Italians have always been my friends, and Victoria, who'd spent much time in Florence, really loved them. We often dined with them and everyone made it plain that, although war seemed imminent, they did not want to fight against us. Goering and a party of generals came to our hotel one day and I well remember the lift boy's disparaging remarks about those confident fellows.

Here we were placed fourth in the Nations Cup, and Mussolini presented us each with a medal. On the last night, after a wonderful ball, we were standing on the stairs with the Polish team when quite spontaneously they filled our glasses with neat gin, no vodka being available. We drank it in one gulp and threw down the glasses. Their glass-smashing custom certainly had a special significance that night: a weird feeling.

We should have left for England early the next morning, but there was some delay because a number of Mussolini's enthusiastic young supporters had seen our car, with those letters G.B. of which we were so proud. I can't believe they'd had the wit to intend it as a jibe against this nation of gardeners, but anyway they'd filled our petrol tank with lawn-mowings.

10

War

In mid-August 1939 Victoria and I motored up to Scotland to stay with How and Sylvia Wiley. How commanded the Leicester Yeomanry, and during the summer I'd visited all the camps of our Brigade: 'war' positively saturated the air, but we still hoped it wouldn't come. He had a small rough shoot and some fishing on a loch. The first evening we fished, caught a few small trout; next day we walked many miles and got a mixed bag. Returned to the hotel, we'd just settled down for supper when the telephone rang, and it was what we all dreaded: mobilisation to start at midnight. We finished our supper, pretending to believe that nevertheless war would not come, packed and motored back through the night to York.

A few days later, on my way to Doncaster, I pulled into a garage and listened to Neville Chamberlain's famous speech. At approximately the same time, the instruction came to Brigade H.Q. that officers like myself holding staff appointments would not be permitted to leave them and rejoin their regiments for six months at least. I knew the Yeomanry wouldn't go overseas to begin with, for horses couldn't be used in Europe, but they were expected to relieve the regular regiments in Palestine, and this did in fact happen in the New Year. The following Sunday, a glorious, hot, sunny evening, Victoria and I were playing tennis with the Diggles when I was called to the telephone—to be told by Northern Command that I must return to my regiment at Colchester immediately. There'd been some changes and I was to go back as second in command. A bitter blow for Victoria: the Inniskillings were the Divisional Cavalry Regiment of the 4th Division, one of the first designated to go overseas. It is difficult now to write of my feelings then. I was a Regular soldier; I belonged to my father's regiment and naturally longed to be back with it and all my friends; on the other hand, Victoria was unwell, with Antony on the way, and our intensely happy life in Yorkshire had to end.

In Colchester the days were ceaselessly busy, packing up, issuing kit, getting the light tanks and carriers ready. Reservists poured in and with what spare time I had I learnt to drive a tank and use the ·505 machine-guns. I was thankful to be so occupied, for although Victoria kept up her spirits

59

wonderfully, we were desperately fond and in love, and the future didn't bear thinking about.

The C.O., Jack Anstice, went ahead to Avonmouth, leaving me to bring the regiment, and early one Sunday morning (everything fateful seemed to happen on a Sunday that year) my tank led the regiment as we rolled out of Colchester Barracks. Down the main road for London, Victoria had parked the car in a side lane and as I passed we waved and I looked away as quickly as I could. Partings were hell. I loved Victoria.

A very odd feeling rumbling through London that Sunday, down Oxford Street and Regent Street. We were the first troops to be on our way, so hardly surprising that waving, curious people lined the streets, wishing us good luck. Now I was thankful to have the goodbyes over, for I knew in my heart I could not have borne to be left at home with a Yeomanry Brigade. Poor Victoria might have denied it, but I believe she was proud really and preferred this to my staying behind. Surely all true soldiers' wives must feel that?

The weather continued gloriously hot, as though to smile brazenly at our leave-taking, and we remained three or four days at Avonmouth, under strict security, not allowed to tell our families where we were, until finally we boarded three ships for an unknown destination. That sea trip was hell, the small merchant ship grossly overcrowded, and out in the Atlantic we proceeded to twist and zigzag to avoid submarines. I was sick all the time and hardly remember anything until we landed. St Nazaire, of course, later became well known as a U-boat base, raided by the commandos; here we unloaded and moved just north to await orders. You could say that we were now ready for war, except that many things happened to be still missing, such trifles as ear-phones for my wireless sets and H.E. for the mortars on our tanks. That was absolutely typical of Hore-Belisha, the Secretary of State for War, who regularly answered questions in the House asserting that the British Army was fully equipped. A steady stream of lies. We stayed there a week or so, continued to train, and did a lot of shooting out to sea using tracer bullets—until stopped because of understandable complaints from local fishing-boats.

Then up to a small village about thirty miles north-west of Lille. I went ahead to allocate our billeting area, setting a pattern which was to continue: i.e. a race with Tommy Arnott, Second-in-Command of the 15th/19th Hussars. I'm afraid I used to get the best area, Tommy being no quicker at this than on the polo ground. Life for the next two months became rather stagnant, an anticlimax after the seemingly purposeful move to the French frontier. We trained and trained, and tried to stave off boredom with football or basket ball and long runs. So I was thankful in mid-December to be sent down for a week's attachment with an Infantry Brigade, about fifteen miles in front of the Maginot Line. This legendary white elephant, extraordinary in every sense of the word, had a series of huge forts built into the hills east of Metz. Woods had been planted on the forward slopes, ostensibly to 'guide' attacks into the cross lines of fire from the various emplacements. These forts held up to five hundred men and in some ways resembled battleships, with a sort of super crow's-nest at the top in which sat the commander directing their highly theoretical operations. The Germans, of course, knew all about each fort, and since these ran in one long thin line they could either outflank or drop behind them. When the attack came on May 10 those proud fortresses never fired a shot. The battalion to which I'd been attached held a four-mile stretch in the front line: the country had been cleared of all inhabitants and platoon posts sited at the edges of the woods. This was no-man's-land; the Germans about four miles away; and both sides used to send out night patrols. The French did little: they slept sound, firmly believing that at any time they could retire to safety behind the Maginot Line.

The Commanding Officer of the East Lancs, a V.C. from the First War, used to allow me to go out every night with the patrols. This was an intensely exciting game: faces and hands blacked, armed with Tommy guns, revolvers, Very Light pistols, and strung with hand-grenades, we'd move silently for three or four hundred yards then lie down to listen. One night, crossing a bridge over a deserted branch railway line, we heard rustling in the undergrowth below; crouching, my heart banged as we waited to fire, for we feared an ambush—until an unmistakable grunt told us there were pigs in the area! And that was the nearest we ever got to any Germans.

Another night, before going off, we were called over to be spoken to by General Alan Brooke, as he then was. Years later, at the European Horse Trials in 1954, I again met that C.O. of the East Lancs. and he told me that Alan Brooke had given him a real rousting, wanting to know *who* the cavalry officer was, going out on patrol (he'd identified me by my revolver being strapped to the leg, as worn in tanks). He was told bluntly that senior officers did *not* go out on patrol.

Early in January I went home on leave, back to Highfield, deep in snow. For days Victoria and I talked and talked—and that might have been the shadow of a premonition of how long we were to be parted. The shooting was marvellous; indeed, one day with Elsey the trainer was, I believe, the best fun in my life when, late morning and afternoon we shot two pheasants, four duck, four snipe, two woodcock and two rabbits. We had good walks through the snow; Victoria well and happy, but Antony looming large, due to join this world in March. That leave, like most, I suppose, ended too soon. We went to London, and when I left the Connaught Hotel at three o'clock one morning and drove to Dover, that was goodbye to Victoria for nearly four years.

So back to the regiment and the monotonous routine of training and contriving to keep the men fit and occupied. Important persons used to visit us, Winston Churchill among them. General Montgomery came, but I fear we did not at that time like him: he only seemed interested in making the men remove their berets, to see if their hair was cut. I kept the blood churning by playing very rough net-ball in the snow, and even finished in the first ten of a regimental cross-country race ('Monkey' Blacker was second, I remember) and felt ridiculously pleased as a man always does when he gives away seven or eight years to the other runners. On March 5 we went out on a night exercise, and I was standing in some cold muddy village talking to Jack Anstice when a despatch rider drew up with a message. It read: 'Major Ansell will take command of Lothian and Border Yeomanry from 0600 hrs March 6.' A complete bombshell. Naturally, I was pleased: I'd never expected to get a command until the war proper started, and at thirty-four I'd be easily the youngest commanding officer in the Army (later on the age dropped considerably, of course). I didn't want to leave the regiment, and I'd always hoped one day to command the Inniskillings; so very mixed feelings.

That night we all slept in a loft, and I woke early feeling awful. I called on the doc., who opened my shirt and laughed: 'You won't take command of the Lothians today. You've got German measles!' The rest of the day was spent 'hopping mad' and drinking endless unwanted cups of tea in an ambulance waiting at the railhead—until a telegram from my Victoria announced the arrival of Antony, to which I replied, 'Well done. Have got Command of the Lothians and German measles.' A magnificent hospital train now trundled a solitary brother officer and myself slowly back to Dieppe. The British Army then had two such trains, so this was a kind of rehearsal of what was to come, but when the Blitzkrieg started neither ever got away. It took more than two days to reach Dieppe, by which time I felt cured, but had to stay in hospital for a week. So I chafed; pondered on my new job. All I knew of the Lothians was that they were referred to as Loathsome and Bloody by their envious fellow Yeomanry regiments.

However, impossible not to enjoy oneself in Dieppe; and the weather being good I would watch the fishing-boats unloading their colourful catch and eat well in small inexpensive restaurants. Cleared of infection, my temperature rose when I learned that the laws of red-tape decreed that I should be taken back to base by train, and proceed to my command from there. When? I asked. Eleven o'clock tomorrow morning, came the reply. That was enough. I telephoned the Inniskillings and got them to pass an urgent message to the Lothians: prompt at nine o'clock the next morning, a new Humber Snipe arrived, and I swept off to take up my new command.

When I reported to the Divisional Commander, Major-General 'Bulgie' Thorne, he explained what seemed to me a very odd situation: I was to take over from Lt-Col Harry Younger, who'd been given the choice of reverting to Major and remaining as Second-in-Command or returning home. He further explained, to my embarrassment, that it would be left to me to send Younger home or keep him, as I wished.

Difficult to imagine a trickier position for a new young C.O., most of whose officers were older than himself, rather inevitably in the Territorials. So I felt nervous when I entered their Regimental H.Q. to be greeted by a young adjutant, Nigel Baird, obviously suspicious of what they'd been sent. Almost immediately things were made smooth for me by the grace of Harry Younger, a quiet, unassuming person, who didn't mind what happened so long as his regiment was well served. We became great friends.

I don't think I've ever worked much harder than in the following few weeks. The Lothians were a splendid regiment, the officers all friends in civilian life, the men of high intelligence and even intellect—most of them from around Edinburgh. And they had to work. They knew virtually nothing: few could even throw a grenade or handle a rifle properly. I had a superb R.S.M. in Mr Kerr, a tremendous disciplinarian; but discipline's not easy in the Territorial Army: it's better to lead than order. Jack Anstice and Herbert Lumsden, who commanded the 12th Lancers, freely lent me instructors wherever needed, and with men of such quality learning was easy. But how stupid is the policy of the British Army. We hang on to our best in each regiment, only sending instructors we don't want to the Territorials, and in each war the best are either killed or taken prisoner within the first few months. When will we learn our lesson?

Something more had to be done to overcome the Lothians' suspicion of me; they always seemed to be expecting me to ram the Inniskillings down their throats. Football is a great prestige-raiser, and the Lothians were good; so we challenged the Inniskillings, holders of the Cavalry Cup. I struck the team off duty for a week and sent them to practise with the 12th Lancers. Win, I swore to myself, we absolutely must. The big day came, and the Lothians ran rings round their opponents. Never did I cheer harder as my rather undersized team tied the mighty Inniskillings up in knots. Jack Anstice paced silently, very silently, up and down the touch-line, and the more I cheered the more he became annoyed, his pacing ever so slightly faster. That win raised the Lothians' morale and, more important, it raised mine, for in their eyes now I really was a Lothian.

In the middle of April, General Thorne told me that we were to join the 51st Highland Division, due to move into action in front of the Maginot Line. My new boss would now be General Victor Fortune. I truly believe that, had we been given another month, there wouldn't have been a better cavalry regiment in the Army: the officers enthusiastic and our men mad keen and highly intelligent. At the time it was regarded as a training exercise, and everyone envied the Highland Division. Little did we realise our fate.

So down to the villages I'd already seen with the East Lancs., and here we were detailed to hold three posts as infantry and provide a tank troop with each of the three forward companies. The rear squadrons took over from the French, who'd been there all winter. Needless to say, they'd done nothing: the would-be trenches weren't dug, merely marked with tape. At about this time I was shown a squadron of the French seventy-five-ton tanks. 'Giants', as their badge symbolised; an elephant rampant. They never became rampant, however. They ran out of petrol before going into action.

Since the outbreak of war the French holding this sector had done little but fire the occasional shell, which undoubtedly suited the Germans, busy preparing for the invasion of Holland, Belgium and the north of France. The country at that time of year had broken out in all its beauty: the shining beech woods, the open hills; but the villages completely deserted. To crown the period of Phoney War, it had been decided, partly for political reasons *vis-à-vis* the French, to send a British Division to this perfect and ironic setting in the Saar. Regimental H.Q. was in the village of Waldweistrof, where Hunting, my soldier servant, found me a nice room which I shared with two families of birds: they nested in the beam above my bed. The French had left the village in a filthy state: even today I occasionally meet men in Edinburgh who are amused to remind me of how I gave orders to 'get that damned place cleaned up at once'. Within a few days muck heaps were squared up, gardens quite tidy and the houses whitewashed. We were all proud of our little village, and though people may wonder, I'm convinced this is good for morale: if you live in filth, morale quickly goes. Also, you must make a sort of 'home' wherever you are.

I soon decided I wasn't going to live on tinned milk, so Hunting took a truck and collected two cows from behind the lines. From then on, whenever we moved, 'the Colonel's cows' came too.

With the arrival of the Highland Division the war became a little less passive: patrols attacking the enemy posts night after night and the Germans retaliating. I loved this life. My regiment was getting invaluable experience. I enjoyed the country while I could. Just before dawn each day, Hunting would call me and we'd set off. As it became light we'd leave the car and walk through the woods to our various posts, the woods full of *lis muguets*, Lily of the Valley, and large wild orchids. Mr Kerr and any trooper with us kept their eyes skinned while I picked hard, and we always had lovely flowers in the mess and my bedroom.

Skirmishing went on, and we had our first casualties. An infantry post had been overrun. We counter-attacked successfully in open country, but lost a tank with two men killed; so early next morning Major Jimmy Dallmeyer, another trooper and I crawled the five or six hundred yards beyond the post, managed to get the dead men out, smash up everything and bring back the wireless set, which was damned heavy. A very tedious crawl. Then a forward post had the first taste of a flame-thrower. An easy matter to knock out the source of the flame, and the next day they brought in the dead German. An enormous cylinder or 'tank' was strapped to his back, with a spray attached rather like what I now use in my garden. A huge man, of course, to carry that weight. I don't think these human flame-throwers were much used, because provided the defenders kept their heads it was suicide. But the Germans often made good use of dogs, that ranged three or four hundred yards ahead of the patrol and as soon as they heard or smelt would return to the handler and point. Difficult to combat, for one couldn't see or hear them at night.

After losing two more tanks at night (the element of surprise had gone and the Germans never now attacked unless well guarded on their flanks by anti-tank weapons) we had to give up this form of counter-attack: with the scarcity of tanks, replacements were only too rare. So this strange interlude in glorious countryside drew to its close. I was happy, the regiment becoming highly trained and used to various forms of fighting—and I can't resist quoting from what Eric Linklater was later kind enough to write in his book *The Highland Division*:

> ... the Yeomanry, under the indefatigable Colonel Ansell—who had a kind of genius for suddenly appearing in the very place where he was needed—had throughout the brief campaign been busy as a maid-of-all-work, as fiercely mobile as His Majesty's destroyers.

On the night of May 9 all hell let loose. Every post of the Highland Division was attacked but not one lost. Next morning we licked our wounds and learnt that the French had fallen back on our right flank—towards safety, they believed, behind their Maginot Line. At midday I stood listening to the B.B.C. news and it was clear the war had really started at last. Orders came for the Lothians to cover the withdrawal of the division, so gladly we were doing our proper cavalry job. In addition I was ordered to rendezvous with the right flank French C.O. and take over on a wide front. I went myself to meet him, and found at the rendezvous not a soul in sight: not even a German. The French had gone.

During the next day we fell back, and I only remember two things: first, sleeping in a wood—it seemed almost sacrilege to let Hunting lay out my sleeping bag, the Lily of the Valley was so thick—second, the ham— Victoria had written saying she'd sent me a ham from Fortnum and Mason. How I found out I don't remember, but I did find out, and that ham was eaten by the Sergeants' Mess! I knew who'd taken it, and punishment was unnecessary, because I told him just what I thought of him. We laughed about it in later years, but . . .

Despite the maddening lack of news of what was happening in Northern France, we realised the big attack had come through Belgium—just as in 1914, as if anyone could have doubted it—and we were involved in a feint in order to hold us: hardly necessary since the French had already disappeared. About May 13, orders came to move quickly to Sedan (north from where the Highland Division had reorganised) which was being heavily attacked. The Lothians covered some thirty or forty miles by road, meeting no opposition, and settled down for the night in a deserted village—not, of course, that we expected it to be anything but deserted. The next morning being a Sunday, I asked our Padre, Padre Rankin, to hold a service. There was no parade, no orders to go, but that small village church was packed, and every man singing. For such is life: when in a crisis we flock to the good Lord. I don't suppose I have enjoyed, if that is the word, any service more. I don't know the name of that village, but I certainly remember seeing a brass plaque in the church, which read: 'To the memory of the U.S. Regiment in this village who were the farthest in advance at the time of the Armistice in 1918.'

The following day came orders for the whole Division to rejoin the B.E.F. —but no one knew where. Harry Younger left with an advance party by road while I took the regiment by train. I remember little except managing to sleep on the floor of my carriage between halts, where we made sure that our mediocre defence against air attack was suitably manned, and that the men weren't off flirting with the local girls. And so we meandered through France with no idea of destination, and neither did we care: exhaustion has that effect. The weather was perfect, news on the B.B.C. was hell. We finally detrained somewhere in Normandy, and, miraculously it seemed, were met by Harry Younger: he, as always, at his most lyrical about the enthralling country he'd driven through.

The Highland Division assembled, and the Lothians were ordered to cover and advance on Abbeville. The Germans had already swept through the town, but had been driven back by part of the Armoured Division under General Roger Evans. So here was my old Colonel and with him Charles Keightley. Home again—but not for long. I sought out the Armoured Division H.Q., and we had a grand reunion luncheon. I was now a 'veteran' and had much to tell, but nevertheless Charles outdid me, recounting how he'd arranged for that Armoured Division to be so well equipped with the newest anti-aircraft guns. He'd seen some Bofors guns parked at a siding in England, had carefully explained to a Railway Transport Officer at Salisbury that these belonged to the Armoured Division, and had just taken them. Some other command was presumably frantically searching for them. How I envied Charles. All we had were out-of-date Lewis guns mounted on anti-aircraft tripods. It was typical of him—and I would have done the same.

II

———— ✦ ————

Débâcle

The lack of news was almost unbelievable. Rumour said the Germans had broken through and over the Somme. The weather had been unusually dry, the river level very low, so nothing seemed more possible. About May 29 I was told to advance on Abbeville and cover a front of some five miles. I was to search out any pockets of Germans and push them back. We met no resistance until almost at Abbeville, held by the Germans and being attacked by the French. On a Sunday, June 1 I think, we got our expected orders to move up to the Somme and cover the withdrawal of the Armoured Division and the French. It appeared most likely the main German attack would come through Abbeville along the coast road; the Lothians were to hold a front of about eight miles on the right of the Division, with the French on my right.

In the early hours of Monday morning I went ahead to find the Headquarters of the French Brigade, part of which we were to relieve. I came to a small country school, and I have always remembered that meeting with the Brigadier: a fine-looking man, dressed in the black leather jacket of the Tank Corps, comparatively young for a French general. He showed me where his troops were, I said I would move up and take over just before dawn. I then enquired whether his troops would still be there or might they already be gone (it had happened to me twice before). He was angry, very angry, and through the interpreter told me that if he said his men would be there, there they would be. Before light broke we moved silently up, to take over from a very efficient French Brigade. Little did I realise that I'd been talking to the future great leader of France: his name was Charles de Gaulle. He certainly made a great impact on me, and I remember noting at the time that he wore one solitary decoration, the Médaille Militaire. It is unique in that it is awarded only on rare occasions to an officer, whereas we have the Military Cross for officers and the Military Medal for other ranks. I think it was typical of de Gaulle's austere showmanship: now we would call it a gimmick, like Montgomery's beret, Churchill's cigar or my ancestor Sir Thomas Picton's going into battle in a top hat.

We had our Regimental H.Q. in a hamlet near a village called Bray—I shall never forget that because the attack came on the 4th: hardly a 'glorious 4th of June'. The tiny house had been left in total disorder, beds unmade, a half-finished meal now rotting on the table. I immediately went up to the forward squadrons: Jimmy Dallmeyer with 'A' on the left, Sandy Usher and 'C' on the right. They were holding high ground overlooking the Somme, but 160 men on a four-mile front with two bridges and the possibility of walking across at almost any point—not the most difficult problem for an enemy to solve. There was thick cover in the Somme valley to make infiltration easy.

We were in touch with both squadrons by wireless and had a link direct to Division. Early on the morning of the 4th Jimmy Dallmeyer came through to say he was being attacked in strength; almost immediately, the same from Sandy Usher. At first light I decided to move out of our village and take up position in the woods just behind. Within minutes of our withdrawal the village had been shelled and bombed. By nine o'clock, 'A' squadron was thick in heavy fighting, Bobbie Dundas and Adam Thorburn-Brown had been killed, and it became obvious that the Germans could not be stopped from passing through. I told Division that we would be unlikely to be able to hold on—only to be told in turn that we must not withdraw before six that evening. I remember thinking, 'Hell, how can we stay here?'

About midday I had my first taste of dive-bombing. A squadron of fighters flew low over our wood, dropped their bombs, then returned to dive and spray us with machine-gun fire. We all lay under any tank or carrier we could find, and at first I was terrified by the screaming of the planes (a good device the Germans had specially fitted, of course), and the noise of the bullets through the trees. With the luck of no casualties from this, I thought we'd better move before they returned—a good thing too: the Germans decided to shell our old position. I then received orders to fall back late that evening and concentrate at the village of Oisement, fifteen miles south. My problem was how to get out, so I went up in a carrier to join Sandy Usher and give him his orders, fully expecting to meet Germans already through. I saw no one, but Sandy had had trouble with the French, or men dressed in French uniform coming up his road—he'd fired to warn them and they'd sheered off south out of our area. Nothing could be done about 'A' Squadron with Jimmy: we had no hope of getting there. I could only tell him that we would cover his withdrawal and he must get out of it somehow to rejoin me at Oisement.

The Covering Squadron rolled into Oisement late that night. We'd had nothing much to eat since dawn and were just about out. I slept on a pew in the church, the first place we found, mistaking it for a school in the pitch dark. Jimmy got back to us with half his squadron: the casualties had been heavy; two troops, one under John Brackley (now the Duke of Sutherland) never got out and were captured. No, not a 'glorious 4th June', 1940, though for that action I later received the D.S.O.

Just before dawn on the 5th, I was woken with orders from General Victor Fortune to hold the village until told to withdraw. The Lothians were to cover the right of the Highland Division and I was to make contact with the French. I went to get my bearings at first light, finding what was in fact a small town, completely deserted, with a railway running north and south; near the station stood three large gasometers. Absolutely flat arable land lay in the direction of the Germans for some eight hundred yards, then a wood. Oisement on a slight hill. Patrols moved out meeting nothing. We searched south seven or eight miles for the French, but never a sign: so obviously *we* were the right flank and all was open beyond us. Another gloriously hot day. We quietly dug in. Regimental H.Q. had moved back with Harry Younger. He found a nice comfortable farm, full of animals, the wretched cows in a bad way, unmilked. Plenty to eat, and my Dispatch Rider soon wrung the necks of all the fine Aylesbury ducks. At least the Germans would not get those.

All quiet—too quiet—and as we slept on and off we knew it would come, for 'B' Squadron, dug in near the railway line, had seen movement in the woods. At about six that evening, the same routine: dive-bombing, followed by scream-diving with machine-gun fire. This time it didn't worry me; in fact I rather enjoyed watching the spray of bullets from a shallow trench. The pattern was fun to see, splayed wide, and one soon realised it would be quite unlucky to be hit. Then came the shelling. Not such fun. Messages kept coming in from the two forward squadrons that they were being thoroughly plastered. We could see that: it was only about four hundred yards away. An hour later I had orders to hold on till midnight, then withdraw through a Brigade of the Highland Division holding a line ten miles to our rear. Once again I remember thinking, 'Hell, what a hope. We'll be overrun.' I went up front to see Watty and Sandy. Oisement hardly a health resort: gasometers blazing, shell-holes for a street and our church flattened with the rest of the buildings. Just as it was getting dark, shelling and strafing redoubled and out from the wood came the German infantry *en masse*—I might have said in a crowd: they could have been leaving a football match.

For a time they made it easy for us: they could never get across that flat open country. We poured out fire with every weapon we'd got. Still they came on; still we stopped them. As night closed in we knew we'd held them up, and at midnight we withdrew.

I was sorry to leave our little farm, and remember it to this day: the orchard, that squat farmhouse with its pond—a timeless contrast to the modern town with gasometers burning well into the night. All the trucks and my car had gone ahead. Last of all, I climbed regretfully into the sidecar (more peaceful than a tank); that sidecar well packed round my feet with white ducks. And rumbled back through the night, thankful to pass behind our infantry for the first time in many days. Sleep was good that night, I don't suppose I'd had more than six hours during the past three days.

And so it went on: no respite for more than ten days. I never got into bed save once and then with my clothes on, and naturally when commanding you cannot let those under you think you are tired. The Lothians' duty was always to cover a retirement, but that wasn't all: we had to send out patrols and constantly try to make contact with the French. I had the most superb regiment, as General Fortune was well aware: he used us to the full. News still sparse, but we understood that Dunkirk was more or less over; we were the only part of the B.E.F. left in France. It's now known that it had possibly been done for diplomatic reasons, as a gesture to the French. Churchill hadn't given up hope of rallying them.

I wrote my letters to Victoria and thought incessantly of the day when I would get home, but quietly I knew we were for it. Sitting under a signpost in the sun, always the sun, how I wished it could rain and slow up the German advance. I was waiting for a divisional conference, with Victor Campbell; now a major-general, he'd been in my platoon at Sandhurst and followed me as High Sheriff of Devonshire (his father was unique in being a V.C. *and* a winner of the Grand National). We talked, and speculated that the Germans had ceased to press the Highland Division because it was too slow—they'd swung south to push through the French; before long they would double back from our capitulating allies to surround us. And that indeed is what happened.

In a small schoolroom Victor Fortune explained that we would now retire to Le Havre. One Brigade under Stanley Clarke was to fall back to cover us. We knew well we didn't have a hope of getting to Le Havre. Stanley Clarke's Brigade in fact got there; we continued slowly, to conform with the French, who had mainly horse transport. The German Air Force watched us incessantly, but never a sign from the R.A.F., and each day the Lothians covered some part of the retreat. I remember being sent to get a territorial battalion of the Royal Scots Fusiliers out: they were Pioneers and too inexperienced to be left behind. We got them out, but I didn't think too much of that job: my men were very weary and had to work from one flank to the other in darkness. Moving back after our withdrawal, we picked up many of these Royal Scots Fusiliers and they sat on the sides of the tanks. Roads were packed with refugees whom we endeavoured to stop, unavailingly. Without doubt many Germans filtered through dressed as civilians.

About this time two naval officers joined Divisional H.Q. to keep in direct wireless contact with the Navy. I mention this particularly for they were both captured by the time we got to St Valéry: the destroyers had no orders and came into Veules les Roses, six miles east.

During the next few days the withdrawal carried on without serious fighting. Each evening the Transport Officer, Joe Hume, found me a temporary H.Q. in some small château, and here I could have my clothes off, get under a cold tap and settle down to a good supper with champagne looted from some cellar. I was fond of that champagne, and Joe being a wine merchant in civilian life ensured he found the best. On the night of the 10th I'd just laid down when a message arrived from Division: as expected, the Germans were now between us and Le Havre. We were encircled. I was to face about, move on a front of eight miles or so and attempt to break through. Our first objective was a narrow river running north/south, and before long I learnt that the leading troop of 'B' Squadron under Sergeant-Major Hogarth had gained contact with the enemy holding this river line. Hogarth put up a magnificent show. His tank was hit, both men killed, the tank caught fire and with both his legs broken he climbed out and crawled into a nearby cottage. His two remaining tanks had been hit and the crews either killed or later made prisoner. Hogarth stayed in the cottage till dark, then with the help of a couple of broomsticks managed to heave himself slowly back towards our lines. He found a British Army truck, round the rear back axle of which a tow rope had become entangled. He crawled underneath and after much tedious labour managed to remove the rope, started up the truck, then by using his hands on the pedals somehow drove it back to us. For this brave and determined example, Hogarth later received the D.C.M.

There was now no possibility of breaking through to Le Havre, and on the following morning we drew back and were told to take up position four or five miles south of St Valéry. At least a French Brigade was believed to be holding on south of us: they would fall back at eight that evening, leaving the Lothians to hold the line until midnight. We would then withdraw and embark at St Valéry. What a hope, thought I.

While our troops moved up I went off with my squadron leaders to look at our positions as from the front, and saw, half a mile away, great masses of men advancing. It was only four o'clock, so thinking the Germans must have broken through we hurried back to the regiment. As this mob approached, we saw through glasses their French uniforms—they'd fallen back four hours early. I shall never forget their panic. Officers on motorbikes, men throwing away weapons or tying white handkerchiefs round the muzzles of their rifles. For all the world like a herd of frightened cattle, and no stopping them.

Evening drew in as we waited for an attack that never came. The Germans were pushing in from the flanks and had St Valéry well covered by artillery fire. Victor Fortune came up to see me and again explained that we must remain there until midnight, then smash up our tanks as best we could, take out our arms and move into St Valéry where we would be the last to embark. Convinced that we would never get away from the port, I asked if we might break up into small parties, after the midnight deadline, and endeavour to escape on our own. It was agreed, but first I had to cover the withdrawal back into St Valéry. The code word would be Tallyho. Victor Fortune hadn't been at his H.Q. for some time, so I explained how the French had 'withdrawn' four hours early. He told me to find the French commander and tell him from General Fortune to order his men to stay in the line.

So off I went looking in the sidecar of my motor-bike, with a liaison officer. It was no easy matter along roads now packed with refugees and French soldiers, but eventually I found the H.Q. in a small orchard looking lovely in the evening sun. Military Police stopped me at the gate and only after a great deal of argument allowed me in. The General, I was told, was waiting to surrender his sword to the German commander (Rommel, as a matter of fact).

I found him in a long low room overlooking the orchard and that same lovely setting sun. A small man, walking up and down like Felix the Cat. He was in Full Dress, with sword and all his medals. I became very angry as he waved away my questions saying he did not know where his troops were and now it did not matter, he wished to surrender. It should be remembered that at this time the French were under the command of Victor Fortune.

At midnight we smashed up our trucks, carriers, tanks, wireless-sets and removed any arms. Worse than the exhaustion was the sense of utter blankness. My orders were to take the men into St Valéry, and I had to, but I never believed the Navy could take us off from there. Now I *know* it would have been better to break up where we were.

In perfect order the men fell in on the road, and moved off in silence towards St Valéry. I was at the rear but we could soon see that the town was being shelled and burning. Down a steep hill into the small fishing town. The pace slowed until we came to a halt. Complete chaos, darkness lit by burning houses, men crouching against any bit of cover. The entire Highland Division was there, and hordes of French soldiers. Then the news passed back through the halted columns that the Navy had not come in: there were no ships. We sat down on the pavement, too tired to think.

I saw and received orders from General Fortune that the surrender would come at 6.00 a.m.; General Fortune had no alternative. Meanwhile the Germans could continue to blast the packed town while we waited for the light.

12

------◆◆◆◆------

Into the Dark

Just before dawn I gave the order, Tallyho. My men were out, exhausted, asleep on the road wherever they'd dropped. And it now began to rain for the first time in weeks: it seemed a fine irony. With Harry Younger I moved around finding as many of my men as possible, endeavouring to cheer them up and urging them to try to get away. I then sat down and sorted out some kit into my pack, putting my best tunic into the bottom. I was wearing an old leather wind-cheater, I remember. Don't really know what my thoughts were, but like any soldier I dreaded the possibility of being made prisoner. I asked who would like to try to get away with me. Harry Younger and Charlie Hopetoun (now the Marquess of Linlithgow) said they'd come, and Waymark with half a dozen other troopers: Jimmy Dallmeyer would take another party. I planned to head south away from the coast, Jimmy to the north-east—he proved more fortunate, for his and other parties eventually got to Veules les Roses, where the Navy picked them up (they went there in lieu of St Valéry). Later Jimmy Dallmeyer was awarded the D.S.O. and bar.

We set off in pouring rain, keeping close to the hedges and trees, and looked for somewhere to lay up and rest till evening. Then we made our mistake. And that is hardly the word. We came across a farmhouse and climbed up into the loft. Had it been fine we would have stayed in the open under a hedge. There was plenty of straw; gratefully we took off most of our sodden clothes, and slept.

A hail of bullets came through the floor and simultaneously the door of the loft flew open and I took the full blast of a Tommy-gun less than ten feet away. We shouted and almost at once it stopped. We then heard voices in French and English below.

What had happened was this: the occupants of the farm had heard us enter the loft and thought we must be Germans; a party of English trying to get away like ourselves came to the farm, probably also looking for shelter, and were told of our presence.

I'd been hit by the blast through the door, I thought my head had gone, and when it stopped I knew I was blind and my hands were numb. During

73

the next few minutes I believed I'd 'had it'. Harry Younger, just behind me, was dead, and Charlie Hopetoun had been hit in the leg. I asked them to leave me and told Charlie to let Victoria know what had happened and 'Tell her I love her.' (In fact he did this, believing I must have died, and for three months Victoria had no other news.)

Waymark, late of the Inniskillings, said he was going to stay with me, and after some argument Charlie agreed to take the others and still try to get away. Waymark tied up my hands and after a while I felt better. We then decided I must give myself up: no alternative. I was blind, both hands in a sorry state, head a mass of blood. I cannot remember much of that long and tedious walk, numbness the primary sensation, but I thought endlessly of Victoria and by now was determined to live. We even wondered whether we might not still get away. Across fields till we came to a railway cutting, through wire fencing, down a steep embankment, over and up the other side. Still vivid the effort of that climbing in my new-found dark. I don't to this day know how far we walked—four or five miles, I suppose—and how Waymark got me there I shall never understand. But I must have been fit, because I'd lost an immense amount of blood, particularly from the left hand.

We hit a road and by chance a French dressing station. Waymark took me in, then blank. I was given morphia, and dressed, and a couple of hours later I was roused by the shouts of Germans. An armoured patrol had arrived. Waymark came to my help, and we were on the walk again—this time back to St Valéry, some seven or eight miles. Two or three miles on, a German truck picked us up and took us into the town. We got out and sat down on the pavement. I'd come quite a circle that day.

It was now well into the afternoon, the town still burning, sun boiling hot. Victor Fortune came over to me, one of the very few remaining, except for stretcher-bearers. We talked a little, till the Germans removed the General and Waymark and left me alone on the pavement. Completely benumbed, still doped with morphia, I cared little about anything. I was a prisoner. I must have fallen asleep, because the next thing I knew a Highlander was talking to me, a stretcher-bearer who'd been sent by General Fortune. They, the wounded and a few British doctors were the only people left. This Jock, whom I met two years later in Stalag 8 at Lamsdorf, was like an angel or fairy godmother. He'd looted some champagne from a burning shop and quickly brought me a bottle. Though warm, in fact almost hot, it was the best bottle of champagne I have ever drunk. I asked the Jock to go through my pockets for my watch (I could do nothing with the bandaged hands). He searched, but literally everything had gone—money, gold pencil and chain, and what I valued most, a silver hunter watch engraved with the crest of the 5th Dragoon Guards, which my father had been wearing when killed at Néry. The French had obviously stripped me at the dressing station.

Later that evening the Germans collected us up and I was made to move into a cellar. Naturally I've no idea what it was like. There were no other English and about six or seven French soldiers, all severely wounded. They locked the door—that seemed hardly necessary—and I lay down on the straw. One of the French told me there was water in the middle: a bucket with a mug. It is difficult to think of that night, and thank goodness I cannot remember. But my despair, well it was almost complete. I could only think of Victoria and the unimaginable future.

During the night we were shelled incessantly, by our own Navy. Why I have never understood. The town had been wrecked, and very few Germans remained. I was the only one able to move, so I felt and crawled my way around, taking water to the French, some of whom were in very great pain. The shelling ceased at dawn. I heard the lock turn and a German looked in with some French woman. They left almost immediately. I knew where the door was, also that it was open, so I fumbled my way there and left too, up the steps and into the street.

I now stood in my leather jacket, trousers and socks. (My boots had gone too.) Feeling my way down the wall I suddenly heard my name. It was Rennie, Major Rennie, who'd been on Victor Fortune's staff. He'd heard about me, and although injured in the leg was out looking for British wounded. Goodness I was pleased to see or rather hear him, and he led me to a small house where the British wounded were being collected and a doctor, Major Walker, had taken command. I found myself with eight or so other officers on the first floor—a real paradise at that moment: straw and a few blankets, though those were hardly needed in the June heat.

The Germans had more or less left. The collapse had been on a scale they'd not anticipated, so the troops had been herded into a field a couple of miles out, and Rommel and his men were pressing on for Paris. The orderlies under Walker collected what stores they could, stretcher-bearers foraged in the deserted streets and wrecked trucks lying about.

Someone found me a razor and a pair of new boots, for which I was prodigiously thankful. After the dressings, the usual cup of tea and some dope. I was out for the next twelve hours. It must have been June 14 when I awoke. I found a tap still running, and shaved with that razor, which I still use—it had been picked up on the beach. Then I proceeded to find out about my companions: none very seriously wounded, except one of my squadron leaders, Sandy Usher, who'd come in while I'd been sleeping. He was in desperate pain, an arm had been shot away, the tourniquet had been left on too long. He now had gangrene and died within twenty-four hours. He lay next to me and, poor chap, was mercifully only semi-conscious.

For the next few days, I lay there and thought, my mind revolving in a hopeless closed circuit. Unless one has ever been a prisoner of war, I think

75

the kind of despair it brings must be difficult to imagine. How much luckier to be a criminal: you do at least know how long you are 'in' for. We didn't know if the Germans would eventually shoot us. We didn't know if the war would last one year or ten. With men wounded and dying, and the depression that breeds, one inevitably expects the worst. But most of all I thought of Victoria, Nicholas and Antony: would I ever see or be with them again? I was determined to get better, and determined to live. Above all, like many others around me, I knew I had to set an example, and however down I might feel must never show it.

During the day we laughed, sang, played games. Some books had been found, and my friends read to me, played those word-guessing games, or the making-up of words from another one. Years later I learnt they used to continue reading while playing these childish games with me. Still the Germans rarely came near us; the orderlies foraged for bully beef, herrings, any tinned rations among the wreckage; and Doc Walker used to take me for walks on the shore. I could talk to him, and listen to the sea. How great my despair, and yet we laughed, joked, and they all pulled my leg about not being able to see. No sympathy ever shown, and how much better it was that way.

About the fifth day, two German doctors arrived with a staff of orderlies. Our doctors had done all they could with their limited supplies but they were unable to do any operations. The German who examined me decided to amputate three fingers. A marquee had been set up outside, and they took me down and sat me on the grass to wait my turn. Before going in, I was put on a stretcher and the French orderlies removed my boots, placing them *on* the stretcher, under my legs. When I stirred out of the operation I automatically felt for my boots—and sure enough they'd gone, for the second time filched by French orderlies when I was unconscious.

The Germans soon departed. Walker meanwhile had made friends with a local civilian doctor who, on learning of my blindness, offered to take me to Rouen to see a French eye specialist. I felt only too grateful, and having got permission from the Germans, he with his wife drove me to Rouen. After a long wait the specialist saw me, but to my disappointment said nothing could be done till the blood behind my eyes had cleared. This had been caused by the blast from the gun. On our way back we stopped at my last H.Q. I particularly wanted to get the fox mascot of my tank. We found the tank, but the fox had gone. We went on to the doctor's house.

I'd been getting much pain in my hand, so after tea he took me into the surgery to have a look at it. He then called to his wife and son, and told me soothingly that he would dress it, as it looked very poisoned. There was whispering, and the next thing I knew the wife and son were holding me while he removed my finger. The pain was intense and I think I half passed out. He then gave me a drink and took me back to my fellow-prisoners. I felt thankful to be with Walker, who was very angry, because both he and the German doctor had been doing all they could to save this remaining finger, the index finger.

For about three weeks our routine continued, the days moving slowly: games, occasional walks on the beach, endless thinking. The French seemed happy, and one evening the town band turned out to play while some of the inhabitants danced. We later learnt these rejoicings were for the armistice that had just been signed. They little realised what was to come. Then finally ambulances arrived and we were removed to a girls' school in Rouen. From there we would be taken by train to Germany. I always remember that night: my hand gave me hell, in a bed suitable for a five-foot girl, not an Englishman of over six feet four. In the morning, when my name was called, the Germans told me to stay. The only one left behind. Was I singled out for some special treatment? If so, what? One had a kind of blockage, thinking about the immediate future. Perhaps we were too frightened, but there was always that dread of death. A German guard then took me, literally, for a walk. I found myself in the Rouen Workhouse, in a ward with thirty or so French officers, shortly joined by two British: Ben Everton-Jones, an R.A.F. pilot shot in the head, and Toby Tailyour, a badly shot-up major of the Seaforth Highlanders. We now came under the care of French military doctors, and before long a young one decided he would have a 'go' at my eyes. I didn't mind. I longed for some treatment. This doctor had read of a new method to break up and disperse blood at the back of an eye. Next morning it started, the treatment to be continued every four days. A solution of sugar or saccharin was injected into each eye. There were no refinements such as local anaesthetics. Ben and Toby stood around and kept up my spirits by characterising the doctor as a good dart player: 'I think this is going to be a double; yes, that's a good one!' etc. As the stuff was pumped in, my eyes blew up like a frog's. The pain was unbelievable.

In between days in bed we walked among the more elderly inmates of the workhouse. All three of us now dressed in a blue workhouse uniform with leather-peaked caps—thank heavens I could not see. The food for us was mainly lentil soup. I loathed it then; now I quite like it. Our fellow-occupants, the French, had money and used to get the charwomen to bring them cheeses, eggs and ham; but none of these luxuries came to us. How we disliked the French: they gave us nothing. By late August we three began to think we'd been forgotten. I'd not been able to write to Victoria. Days drifted slowly by, we laughed together, kept up each other's morale, but alone our thoughts were very different.

America, of course, was not in the War, yet working in France at that time under the International Red Cross was an American ambulance unit. They

77

were driven by girls and went wherever required. One day, three of these ambulances arrived to start evacuating the more seriously wounded French to Paris. Orders were given that the English were not to be removed.

I was still in bed having those infernal injections. Toby and Ben, always on the watch, were delighted to give me news of a new arrival in our midst, for among the drivers was a particularly glamorous girl, Jean Preece. Ben talked to her and soon found that her brother had played polo with me on Long Island in 1935. So Jean came to see me. At last we had contact with the outside world, and I cannot convey the suppressed excitement of that. It was agreed that she and Polly Peabody (an English member of the American unit), equally glamorous and adventuresome, would take me to Paris.

Ben and Toby found me a French soldier's cap and top-coat, and next day, dressed for the part, I was taken down by them and steered into the front seat of Jean's ambulance. German guards at the gate checked us, I kept my mouth shut, and we were through. The road to Paris; I might get treatment for my eyes; I wanted my sight. On arrival at the French Military Hospital, the Val de Grâce, I sat still without speaking while Jean explained that she had orders to take this blind Frenchman to the American Hospital. The German guards did not query it, and almost unbelievably I soon found myself in a lovely room, between clean sheets on a comfortable bed for the first time in over three months. Although running a great risk, Dr Jackson had immediately agreed to take me in. Next day Jean and Polly went back and transported Toby and Ben in the same Pimpernel fashion, and there were three new inmates, Mr Ansell, Mr Tailyour and Mr Everton-Jones at the smart modern American Hospital on the outskirts of Paris.

13

Paris

From a bed of straw, to the workhouse, to one of the most expensive nursing homes in Europe: I did enjoy the piquancy of that. But Doctor Jackson was taking a great risk, in Occupied Paris. My 'Sister', a huge, overpowering, humourless Latvian by the name of Miss Matherson, took charge, and Dr Hartmann the eye specialist prescribed treatment. His diagnosis confirmed that of the doctor's in Rouen—nothing to be done until the blood in my eyes had been absorbed—so back to those injections. Only once a week though, with the refinement of hot swabs to lessen the pain. After each one I had to stay in bed for three or four days till, about the fourth day, I miraculously seemed to be able to see a little more. I longed for the injections, could have borne almost any pain: all I wanted was my sight. Dr Hartmann stopped them after eight weeks, telling me that I'd already had twice as many as a normal person could be expected to stand. I could now see a little out of one corner, and I began smoking in order to watch the smoke out of the side of my left eye. It was thrilling.

This must have been well into October. News of the Battle of Britain reached us. Day after day the bombers flew overhead on their way there. It was hard for those of us captured not to feel bitter: we believed we could have got away with the greatest of ease, and had been made the victims of a futile diplomatic move. We loathed it all, and could never forget that we'd been ill prepared and badly equipped in spite of Hore-Belisha's assurances that the Army was ready.

Visitors used to come to the hospital, but none had so far been allowed to see us. Then one day a French lady appeared, and she asked me if I wanted to get a letter to my wife. Suspecting she'd probably been sent by the Germans, I said no. Later she returned bringing Henri Couturié and Teddy Rasson—I'd played polo with them—who explained that the lady, Madame Tiberghine, was a cousin and to be trusted. In the months to come she proved a true friend to me and subsequently played a quite prominent part in the French Resistance.

So I tried to write my first letter to Victoria. It was agony: the lines went everywhere, and I had so much pent up I wanted to say. These letters were given to an engine-driver who hid them in his coal tender until over the border into Vichy France: from there they looped home via Spain and Portugal. Victoria couldn't read my handwriting. She even sent up to experts at the War Office who also failed to decipher it.

One of our visitors was a priest from the Irish Embassy. I asked him if he knew Dan Corry, and 'Why surely,' he replied, 'the show-jumper.' That was enough for me, and I begged him to slip a note in the Embassy bag saying, 'Tell Dan Corry to let Victoria know Mike is all right.' Dan got it, and telephoned our house at Malton, but Victoria had meanwhile gone to live at her brother's in Wiltshire; a message came there from the police asking her to telephone the Dublin Exchange. It took six hours to get through because of an air raid, and when she finally succeeded the line was so bad that about the only recognisable words were 'Vic, Mike is all right.' Victoria didn't know if I was in Ireland, in France, in Germany or in limbo—but at least I was still alive.

That period at the American Hospital felt weird. It was certainly unique for prisoners: the Germans demanded a list of patients, and Dr Jackson had to admit who we were. A German officer occasionally came to see us, and although we never agreed to parole, we accepted that we should not try to escape while there. Outwardly our morale was high. We walked in the little garden together, still dressed in our Rouen Workhouse blue. My left eye was slowly getting better. We played backgammon, and I learnt to knit: a very gay nurse, Thérèse de Villers, helped me and bought me wool. So the days glided by, but we felt sure that as soon as the Germans became organised after their unexpectedly swift advance, anomalies like us would be rounded up.

It would have been mid-November when an order came that Ben Everton Jones must be ready to leave for Germany the following day. He'd been pondering the risk of escape for weeks: not risk to himself, but we all feared retaliations on the other severely wounded in Paris if we 'abused' our privileged positions (which really enjoined a tacit parole on us). Toby and I knew our turn couldn't be long, and sure enough it came a few weeks later. Before leaving, the usually impassive Miss Matherson beamed through her pebble-thick glasses and begged me for a photograph. I got a beautiful print of my skull from the X-ray department, showing the thirty-odd bits of metal in it (they're still there). 'Oh, Colonel,' wailed the dear Latvian, 'you would do that!' But I had put an ordinary one in the envelope as well.

Toby and I were taken to the Hôpital Bégin, a large, gaunt Military Hospital built at the time of the Franco-Prussian War. Grounds were spacious, as an estate agent would say, walks shaded by lime trees, I think. But this time we were surrounded by barbed wire. I remember little of that place: about eighty of our countrymen, all severely wounded, had been collected and designated unfit to travel to Germany 'as yet'. Toby and I had a room to ourselves and a perfect nurse: French, with a quite unpronounceable name; she always wore an apron with a gigantic pocket in front, so we dubbed her 'Kangaroo'. Ever full of good humour, she was happy to pick up my interminable dropped stitches, and we soon taught her English (easier than learning French). We now fondly hoped, and were constantly being told, that we would soon be repatriated in exchange for German prisoners under the terms of the Geneva Convention. Dr Hartmann continued to visit me weekly. My sight was getting better, and he thought that although both retinas were badly split I still might improve a little more, if only I could rest. So I spent most of the day in bed. Visitors were allowed twice a week for the French soldiers, but they were forbidden to speak to the English. Nevertheless the Frenchwomen used to sweep straight up to us, bringing gifts of eggs and cheese: they were quite fearless, and feeling against their own menfolk ran high at the time. The Germans, who can't bear to be disobeyed, moved among the women taking their names and addresses—I imagine they mostly gave false ones. Madame T. came regularly, and Thérèse and I conceived a great urge to get out into Paris for a day. Dr Hartmann provided an elaborate pass—to go to an oculist to be fitted with spectacles—and either Henri or Teddy Rasson brought clothes. The day arrived and Thérèse steered me through the gates again disguised as a French soldier.

We took the *Métro*, and I remember feeling conspicuous because of my height in a carriage full of German soldiers. I'm sure they took no notice whatever. I felt so free, like a child being taken out for a treat. We went to a café after the oculist, and when I got back through the guard without questioning, I thought how brave T. and Thérèse were: they didn't care a damn for the Germans.

In March about seventy of us left for another Military Hospital, the Val de Grâce. The Commandant told me the Germans were sending us to Switzerland next day: a typically frightened French colonel, he said I must sign a parole, as the senior officer, for all the men. I told him to go to hell, it was *his* duty to the Germans to guard us. That evening T. appeared, like the sorceress she was: she'd brought clothes, and tried to persuade Toby and me to walk out. But I knew I could not, for fear of reprisals on others. So the following day we hoped and wondered, till after luncheon the Commandant summoned me to say we would leave that evening. Where? Switzerland, he felt sure. With an ingratiating smile. How thankful he must have been that no one had escaped.

At a Paris station, presumably the Gare de l'Est, we boarded a magnificent hospital train, quite patently window-dressing by the Germans to show the French how well English prisoners of war were being treated. Supper was served in our bunks, and I settled down to knit. I pushed the bell above my head, and when a typically stern German sister appeared I asked her to pick up my dropped stitch. My friends fell about laughing as she furiously grabbed and picked up the impossible Englishman's stitch. It was good to laugh, for when light came we were plainly heading north-east, for Germany.

The train halted at a small country station that afternoon, and the comfortable glamour immediately vanished. A truck for those who couldn't walk or hobble, the rest marched to their new home.

14

⟶◆◆◆◆◆⟵

Treysa and Spannenburg

Treysa, between Frankfurt and Kassel, our abode a sort of villa standing on the hill; only a five-yard-wide path between it and the high barbed wire. I shared a room with five or six others. In the morning we got up, someone fetched a jug of ersatz coffee, bread and margarine. On Sundays we were spoilt with honey: honey which no fly could be persuaded to come near. We shaved, we made our beds, we existed. We walked endlessly backwards and forwards round the house, while Hitler's *Jugend* tried to charm us with their marching songs. Always a splendid luncheon to look forward to: usually a bucket of turnip soup and another of boiled potatoes—the latter were carefully divided and we found it wise to save one or two, because when the evening soup and ersatz coffee came we were really very hungry. We weren't allowed to write home. There were no letters or Red Cross parcels.

One day in April, we knew something was going on: a smiling German Commandant appeared to say that a Red Cross Commission was expected. They were to decide who should be repatriated. The Geneva Convention clearly stated that those completely unfit to fight should be repatriated, irrespective of numbers: if so classified you were known as a '*Grand Blessé*', or what we called a D.U.—Damned Useless. I appeared before a board of three, among them a Swiss and a Swede, and after questioning was I believe marked D.U. Before the Commission left they asked me, as the senior officer, if I had any requests. I explained that we received no post and had no 'opportunity' to write. They questioned the German Commandant, then stated that the Red Cross would be informed where we were, and that our letters must be posted. That was a great boon: to exercise oneself in writing in such circumstances can be very consoling.

In late May or June 1941, Treysa had its first excitement. From the top rooms of our villa one could see the main line from Frankfurt running due east, and now a steady stream of troop trains and goods traffic, guns, lorries and tanks passed along. I hadn't known, but before the war certain officers had been trained in the use of codes for these occasions. We had one such, and from the start of this flow everything was counted and reported back in our letters. Whether they were of any value I've no idea, but it did wonders for our morale. Day and night we kept constant watch, excited to see the smashed trucks and tanks soon returning. It was, of course, the start of the Russian offensive.

Quite suddenly they moved us forty miles south of Frankfurt to another hospital (so called), where at least there were five British Army doctors. Red Cross parcels had begun to arrive, and with tea, chocolate, tinned milk, raisins, a tin of fish and one of meat, possibly butter and dried apricots— well, it was manna from heaven. If one came every ten days we managed comfortably. One cannot exaggerate the difference getting letters from home made. *Our* writing allowance was two letters and four postcards a month.

All in this camp had been severely wounded; there were constant amputations. But the morale of the men was so superb that it certainly made a really excellent rehabilitation for me. Here I met Guardsman Doy, severely wounded in the face and almost blind. The Germans thought he *was* blind, but whenever one approached he had just enough sight left to lash out and hit him with his stick. Twice they sent me to Frankfurt University Hospital: pleasant excursions, which gave us a much-needed something to talk about. In the streets of Frankfurt, I walked in the gutter while my two armed guards strode along the pavement. I used to see a specialist, but nothing new came of it.

So long as we remained in these hospitals we kept the hope of being repatriated at any moment. Late in September they told us our place was required by the German Army. Officers like myself, not receiving treatment, went to Oflag 9AH, Spannenburg, a small country town just north of Kassel. Senior officers lodged in a pre-war forestry school on the edge of the town, junior officers in the Castle, a most forbidding pile at the top of the hill—it had been used for P.O.W.s in the 1914 War and I'm glad to say the Americans blew it up in 1945. They must have blown away a deal of unpleasant memories. The lower camp was grossly overcrowded but nevertheless quite bearable; indeed it was picturesque, with a river and plenty of trees. We now gave up hope of repatriation and settled down for a life—one, five, ten years? No one dared to think. The secret was to keep oneself fully occupied, and fortunately I never seemed to have time to spare. My friends read to me, I knitted, we all organised courses. There being some two hundred officers, many of them Territorials, meant we could offer courses in almost anything. Bede Cameron and Nat Kindersley (who'd both of course show-jumped with me) and I organised one on equitation. I shall always remember lecturing on the Horse Show of the future, because it was then that I began putting my ideas in order to promote show-jumping as a spectator sport after the War. Several painted, some did the most superb petit point, and one Colonel Peppie, a Horse Gunner, made a complete set of fishing equipment. He managed it like this: each day an army wagon arrived with our black bread and dried fish, and while they unloaded, Peppie pulled a few hairs from the tails of the two horses; with these he plaited himself a line exactly as it used to be done in the old days; he got some hooks, and feathers to tie his flies, and on one of our walks (D.U.s were permitted those) we found him a suitable bit of ash to make a rod. I knew how to make nets, so that was done too.

Once a week the Germans allowed us to exercise on the local football ground, and while the majority played rounders or some such, Peppie fished—so that many of us had an excellent supper that night. Alas, when the Germans discovered their trout were being poached, it stopped.

One of the major occupations, of course, was planning escapes. Groups made various things: civilian suits from blankets carefully scraped down with a razor blade, maps received in gramophone records from England were copied, passports forged and teams in rota tunnelled or watched. A long tunnel was dug and all the soil carried up in cardboard boxes and stored under the roof. They had bad luck though: the tunnel flooded and could never be completed.

In late October 1941, after a month of rumours, they suddenly announced that the eight of us listed as *Grands Blessés* were to be repatriated. I'd hardly dared to hope, and, however one's heart jumped at the thought of home, there was now regret almost amounting to a sense of guilt at leaving friends behind—to a blank or ominous future. The Germans were at their peak in the fortunes of war. Would I really see Victoria and the boys? Always the mind checked at that image: you could never be sure. But that night, with the help of Douglas Thompson and my room-mates, I got together what little I wanted to take, proudly packed my knittings, and any odd picture of the camp. They gave us a rousing send-off next morning, and after a day in the train we arrived at a transit camp: others had already been brought from various camps and hospitals—about two hundred and forty in all. Conditions were very primitive, but I doubt if anyone cared. Early the following day we had a short service, grouped inside the wire, and here we took Communion, giving thanks that at last we should be with our families. And soon a superb hospital train, two of them, in fact, were speeding west; and we felt sure, dared to be sure, that the Germans would never be so lavish were we not going home.

15

Deceptions

Late evening of the second day we sat down to supper in a school somewhere in Rouen. Cloths had been laid, and flowers on the dining-tables: demonstrably the Germans meant us to leave with good impressions. A charming Cavalry colonel, Oberst Martin, was in charge. Very correct and good-looking. The exchange would take place within three days, he told us, via Dieppe and Folkestone. The third day came and went. A hitch, they said. Suspecting the whole thing was off, several prepared to escape. An electric clock in the school tower suddenly stopped; I soon learnt why: the magnet had been removed to make compasses. Days passed, table-cloths became dirty and were removed, the flowers died, and neither replaced. After a fortnight of excuses they finally told us the repatriation was off, the reason given being that some German prisoners had been harshly treated in Russia. The disappointment was desperate, but we did not show it. We cursed the Germans, and felt particularly bitter on learning that our German opposite numbers had even been put on the boat at Folkestone. Later we heard that the Germans, in direct contravention of the Geneva ruling, had stipulated a one-for-one exchange; and there weren't enough German *Grands Blessés* in England. It had been even worse for my Victoria, because she had been told I was coming home. She had her hair done, flowers in the house, and the two boys all excited until, almost unbelievably, she heard on the B.B.C. News at six o'clock it had all been called off. Shattering.

Those, like myself, physically fit moved into a camp in the middle of the Rouen race-course; bed cases went straight back to Deutschland, and one poor man, unable to bear it, committed suicide from the train. Our new camp was 'delightful': unlined Nissen huts, without flooring, and it turned out to be a pretty cold November. Depression didn't help, but we never showed it, and a glimmer of hope remained so long as they didn't send us back to Germany. One morning after roll-call the commandant, Oberst Martin, asked me, 'And how is the Cavalry Club?' Naturally rather surprised, and expecting him to tell me it had been flattened, I replied, 'Very well, and I'm sure very full.' He then told me he was an honorary member, and had been since his days as A.D.C. to the Kaiser, then the Colonel-in-Chief of the Royal Dragoons.

Early in December my sight became very much worse; I was again almost blind. Our doctors approached Colonel Martin, who promised them he would do everything he could to help, and sure enough I was suddenly told to pack. As so often in the past two years, the goodbyes to one's friends were horrible; the unknown was frightening, but always the hope I might get my sight back made any move worth while. Two guards took me to Paris by car, to a German military hospital. I had a small room to myself, which I was never allowed to leave: not that I wanted to, for I spent the next fourteen weeks in bed. Being the only 'foreign' patient, a guard was posted at my door each night, and the Under-Officer removed my trousers and boots—which I never wore, being permanently in bed. Dr Meyer, who tried to do so very much for me, was a top-class eye specialist; he'd had a large practice in Bremen before the War and had frequently read papers at Aberdeen and Edinburgh Universities. After a week's preparation the first operation took place and I remember my relief that at last something was being done—also a break from the usual monotony. Only local anaesthetics are used in this kind of thing; consequently one knows what's going on. In my sort of case the retina is burnt or scarred in certain places with the hope that, healing, it will tighten up and return to its original position. An intriguing part was the smell of burning flesh.

I honestly think those next four months were my most difficult time as a prisoner. It required some determination and faith not to go off my head. There were four operations, each a failure, after which my eyes were bandaged and I had to lie flat with my head between sandbags. The nurse fed me, I couldn't shave or clean my teeth; but I could use my arms, and knitting saved my reason. Dr Meyer was an exceptionally nice person; he talked English perfectly, and he understood the mental strain one had to endure, so a young German sailor was allowed to sit and talk with me. This suited us both: for me the hideous monotony was attacked, and he expressed himself delighted to have a chance to improve his English. Just before Christmas Meyer got permission for dear Madame Tiberghine to visit me. My joy was unbelievable. They allowed her to stay an hour or so, while a stolid guard with rifle and fixed bayonet stared at us, not understanding a single word. I never ceased to be amazed by her courage, for these visits now made her a marked woman with the Gestapo. She was always gay and sympathetic and optimistic, and, goodness knows, we had need of optimism when every hour or so Lord Haw-Haw drawled out some petrifying bit of news: we were pushed back in North Africa, our ships sunk in the Mexican Gulf and then Pearl Harbor. One had to be a fanatic to convince oneself that we would finally win, and above all to conceal one's fears from the

Germans. I longed for what I called the T. days (she came twice a week); I longed for Meyer to come in: he always joked, and loved to tell me of his hare shooting. I thought and dreamt of Victoria, and my home, praying and knowing I would get there one day, but when evening came I was thankful to stick out my leg from under the sheet and get a jab of morphia. It's easy to understand how some take to drugs: with that jab I knew I'd have peace for a few hours.

After any sudden move it always took weeks for letters from home to catch up, and equally I knew how worried Victoria would be by the renewed silence. So imagine my relief when Oberst Martin arrived one day from Rouen with a pile of the precious things. Martin spoke English perfectly, hardly surprising when I learnt he'd been educated at Rugby. He was reading me Victoria's letters, and suddenly said my name was familiar—had my father been in the Cavalry? It then came out that he'd written the official German history of the Battle of Néry, 1 September 1914. These so-called coincidences are strange, when we seem to have a brief glimpse of how all the people in our lives are mysteriously joined together. Colonel Martin was very distressed about the War, and particularly about the repatriation failure —he had, I believe, only come back into the Army specifically to try and bring that off. He once said to me, 'If you are really worth what I believe, you, like many others I hope, will only remember the good things.' That is profoundly true, I think, and at the risk of sounding pompous I'll say that *magnanimity* is the least-prized virtue in the world today.

Not quite sure how I managed it, but I had some money, and on March 26, our mutual birthday, I sent my young sailor to buy flowers for T. and take them to her flat. T. had an old French maid, Germaine, who delightedly welcomed him, and not understanding English, thought he must be an escaped British prisoner *en route* through France. She took him in, but to his surprise and horror pushed him into a cupboard and locked it. Fortunately T. returned from shopping soon after, read my note and immediately twigged. The poor young man was released and he never said a word; he didn't even tell me of the incident, so proving himself more of a friend than I'd believed. But I realised how very stupid I had been.

I'm sure I might have escaped with the help of T. and her friends, but always there were the possible sufferings of the other wounded to consider.

About a fortnight after the final operation Meyer told me he was going on leave but would soon be back. He believed I was getting better. I never saw him again, because within twenty-four hours the Gestapo had arrived. I suppose I should interpolate here that, apart from Meyer personally being a nice man, the German doctors were naturally interested in such a case as mine, particularly in war-time. I mean, if you had both your legs blown off, that was, well, straightforward, but if you were shot through the head or in the spine something might be learnt. And that is not cynicism. Anyway, the Gestapo had little time for such sophistications, and during the afternoon two of them walked into my room, demanded to know what I was doing there, and told me to pack as I'd be leaving for Germany that night. I'd hardly been out of bed the past ten weeks, but with the help of my sailor friend put together what little I had. At eight that evening an officer and two guards took me to the station. The guards helped me and carried my pack and suitcase as far as the barrier: beyond, a German troop train, and no more help once out of sight of the French. With fixed bayonets the guards hustled me into a third-class carriage while the officer left—to travel first-class, naturally. The wooden seats of the continental third-class were hardly famous for comfort, and when we arrived at Berlin twenty-four hours later I felt pretty dreadful. I particularly couldn't stand the weakness, after months in bed. We changed stations and travelled another twelve hours, finally stopping at Lamsdorf, east of Breslau, where they ordered me out on to the deserted platform, told me to pick up my kit and walk. After a three-mile march through quite deep snow, the gates of a prison camp opened and almost within seconds I was surrounded by Sergeant-Major Campbell and others of my own men. I just cannot ever express my feelings, but honestly thought, 'Thank God, I am safe with my own regiment.'

16

The German Tour

Damn the Germans and thank heavens I was here! My troopers picked up my kit, ignoring the German officer and guard, and steered me away to the hutted hospital. Lamsdorf was a Stalag: i.e. for other ranks as distinct from Oflag, for officers only. Here I linked up with Major Charters, a first-rate eye specialist. They quickly got me into bed, warm and comfortable, and I certainly slept well that night. Charters soon got to work, although he had little in the way of instruments; but he decided to try a different treatment, and after a fortnight's rest started a course of injections. Once a week I submitted, and within an hour my temperature rose to 103 or 104, the bed shook, sweat poured, and not until the heat subsided did Charters come in, for I used to curse and declare I would never go through it again. The object was to try to remove the clots of blood from my eyes, and I used to think I did see better. Mostly wishful thinking, I suppose; but I've always been an optimist, and convinced myself that I would not only see again but get full vision back. It was the only way to live.

I didn't remain there long. Off we went again, this time to a lovely hospital in Bavaria: as one might say, from John o' Groats to Land's End—only it's farther. And there I found many of those who'd been in Rouen: could we again be due for repatriation? After two days only they shunted me back to Spannenburg, Oflag 9 A/H, with a group of other officers.

Little had changed. I shared the same room with those I'd left so hopefully yet guiltily eight months before. The courses still went on, and I learnt more about horticulture, genetics and botany. Now it must have been May 1942, when the Germans seemed to become more petty over reprisals: many quite childish and irritating. The one thing we all longed for was news from home—so one morning we were treated to a long tirade about the harsh way the British had treated German prisoners: from now on we would be permitted no letters. This announcement was greeted with cheers and jeers, as always on such occasions, but we'd been hit in one of the softest spots. Shortly after, the Commandant told in ringing tones of the terrible way German prisoners had been treated *en route* from North Africa to Australia or India: German officers, he fulminated, had had their marks of rank removed as souvenirs—by sailors. From now on, British officers were to remove all badges of rank and medal ribbons. More cheers. Worst of all was the sudden removal of all razors, books, eating utensils, towels and soap. So we ate with our fingers, through our beards, and contrived to employ our time without books and writing materials. Much to our amusement, Nat Kindersley pulled his sweater to bits and with a pair of makeshift needles reknitted it. After a month or so a 'beard' show was arranged: prizes for the best beard, the most grotesque, the most insignificant, and the Commandant was invited to present them. Needless to say, he didn't come, but next day the reprisal was withdrawn. The Germans were never allowed to get away with it. Once that same Commandant had everyone called out, to inform us that two young officers had failed to salute him; threats of future punishments were greeted with cheers and catcalls, but after that two young officers always awaited his arrival at the main gate, saluted as he entered, and followed wherever the Commandant went, saluting at every opportunity. If he went to his office, two more waited for him at the door; if he went to speak to a guard, a pair followed saluting behind him. If he went to the lavatory they were waiting to salute when he came out. The effort to maintain a little dignity in his fight against boiling rage was apparently too wonderful to see.

Glorious weather that summer. Life dragged wearily, monotony broken only by reprisals and attempts to escape. Not one succeeded in my time: the river curving round the camp made it extremely difficult. Peter Dollar's effort ended when he hammered a hole through the guard-room wall, where a guard sat waiting for him. Then one evening in September they told me to pack once again. Going alone, I knew it couldn't mean repatriation, and expected to land in another hospital. Berlin this time, it turned out.

In one sense, never a dull moment; and leaving Spannenburg I settled with my two guards in the third-class carriage reserved for British prisoners and passengers accompanied by dogs. As soon as we were seated and the guards had fixed their bayonets, I felt around for my haversack, gave an excellent piece of chocolate to a dog or two, and settled down to knit. Throughout the journey it never ceased to amuse the civilian occupants and to embarrass the guards. The more they became embarrassed, the more I knitted.

I knew we'd struck a good patch again, because as in Paris a car took me from the station to the Tempelhof, possibly the largest German military hospital. A comfortable room to myself, with an excellent medical orderly who'd been head waiter in one of the big Berlin hotels. He was superb, and in spite of the War his training never left him: always calling me sir. Had I been able to see, I'm sure I would have enjoyed watching him bow. There was the same ridiculous routine each evening of my trousers, boots and braces being removed by the Under-Officer and his underlings. I was here for examination by one of the greatest German eye specialists, but he quickly decided he could do no more than already had been done. Two highlights of this short visit: I received a note from Hasse, who jumped with the German team in Rome just before the War; he'd been severely wounded on the Russian front, and heard from the sister of my arrival. He asked to see me, but alas that was *verboten*. However they allowed us to write to each other, and I'm sure we both felt the same: how futile it all seemed. Later Hasse was, I believe, killed on return to the Russian front. The second highlight came as I was about to leave: for the first time ever the Germans decided a colonel should have a soldier to carry his kit, so a young private was collected from a small P.O.W. camp in Berlin. Off we went to the station, as always no idea where we were bound—and it really didn't matter so long as I had a British companion. Those excursions to hospital alone were hell. As we trundled through Germany I thoroughly enjoyed that young cockney's company: he had many good stories. There had been only about a hundred in his Berlin camp, and they were made to work, breaking up lorries, tanks and cars from the Russian front. They immediately removed anything conducive to their future comfort—springs for their beds, shaving mirrors, reading-lamps with batteries, all were part of the loot. From time to time the guards made a fuss about it, whereupon our soldiers refused to do any more work and just stretched out on their bunks. The guards would then arrive, start shouting and letting off their rifles through the roof, until, seeing it had no effect, they would ignominiously have to leave. After a few hours our men returned to work, but I doubt if the Wehrmacht ever salvaged anything of value from that break-up yard.

On arrival at Kloster Heina, I was met by Charters, who'd also been moved and was the British M.O. in charge there. An exceptionally comfortable place this, with one hundred and twenty wounded, among them twenty or so blind or nearly blind. The building was in fact a lunatic asylum: only a wire fence separated us from the inmates. I shared a nice room with two others: one a Captain Halloway of the Merchant Navy who'd been blinded and severely wounded when his ship sank off the South African coast. Over sixty and a man of splendid courage, at times in great pain which he never showed, and always the first to stop anyone expressing bitterness at their miserable lot. He had a great sense of humour, was very well read, and therefore interesting; and luckily we remained together until we went home. The Germans left us alone except for their unpleasant Commandant: after the War he received a short sentence as a War Criminal.

A small centre for badly wounded, and particularly the blind, had been set up here, with the Marquis of Normanby the force behind care of the latter. Thanks to his determination, braille books, cards and typewriters had been sent out through the Red Cross, and consequently those blind were really well occupied learning to use them.

We were told that we'd remain here until repatriated. Though inevitably a bit sceptical about that, we did know from our wireless set (hidden in a medicine ball) that things had started to go well for us, which would mean a lot of German prisoners. So, grounds for hope. Several officers occupied the third bed in our room: Godfrey Cromwell, who'd been captured at Calais and had the distinction of reading his obituary in *The Times*, and finally Ossie Younger, who'd lost an eye and been captured at St Valéry. I soon got in touch with T. in Paris: she sent me a few gardening tools—while Victoria managed to get me seeds of annuals through the Royal Horticultural Society and the Red Cross. Our compound being ideal for a garden, we soon made some good flower-beds with the help of the men, and I doubt if I've ever had better annuals—there were so many of us that every plant could be lovingly protected. We cut the grass with scissors, and Oswald Normanby and I collected sheep droppings from the road on our walks. All in all, a comfortable and very artificial life, learning to type, knitting, talking to friends, gardening. Early to rise, early to bed, hair cut, boots always polished, discipline, morale, cleanliness, and never did we look glum or show we minded in front of others. For we so longed to be doing something worth while, and knew we were quite useless. All I could do was ensure I didn't go off my head, and try to help others.

The soldiers were superb. The Commandant would sometimes come into the compound, shouting and screaming hysterically because some wounded man hadn't saluted. Whistles blew, while all the soldiers did was to shout 'Half time, ref . . . Send him off . . .'

Christmas came—my fourth away from home—and dear T. sent a small Christmas tree. I encouraged the men to decorate; they made the most wonderful things out of old tins. T. also sent a parcel of candles and ornaments for the altar, draped in a scarlet blanket, in a ward we used for Services. It all looked glorious. My thoughts were only of home; my friends' likewise, I am sure; and in that period when we all take stock, between Christmas and the New Year, I wondered how much longer I would have to keep it up. For make no mistake, far the hardest part in this kind of life is the pretending that one does not mind. Morale, morale and more morale: because those who failed could never forgive themselves for it. As the Senior British Officer I simply could not be allowed to fail in that duty.

Came January and February, came the snow, then spring. Four winters away. Would there be a fifth? Constantly we had to tell ourselves how lucky we were to be comfortable at least. We knew we would win, the tide now running inexorably against the Germans; but in defeat would they finish us off too? Now if a German shouted, the British soldier would produce a dirty piece of paper and, with a policeman's dignity, slowly pretend to take the sentry's name and number. The German understood only too well. But what would be our fate?

From time to time new wounded arrived—at this oasis—the largest influx after the Dieppe fiasco, which cost the Canadians so dear. Five or six of them joined us, very severely wounded. They were bitter, convinced the raid had merely been badly prepared and ill-timed. Some of them sat late in our room, arguing about Great Britain, the British Empire and so forth. The old sea captain, who'd suffered more than most, laughed and tied the Canadians up. He knew his history and always won.

In October 1943 it was suddenly announced we would be going home the following day. So once more the awful farewell from those on the repatriation list to those who had to stay. That evening I sat in the compound with Oswald Normanby, on the stones surrounding our garden, and we discussed the past three years. What truly had been lost? What gained? Would we ever know? Could we ever? Of one thing we were certain: we'd seen every type of man in adversity, and we thanked God we were British. The British soldier had stood out, always clean, shaved when possible, and he never let it be seen he was down. The other nations simply could not compare—and we'd seen French, Belgians, Russians, South Africans, Australians, Canadians and Poles. I know that the English have a tendency to think highly o themselves, or had, in the recent past, but I'm sure that anyone with experience of the prison camps would agree that what I've said is unarguable.

We boarded a train early next morning—and sat in it for six hours, wondering why it didn't start. Then the inevitable: there had been a 'hitch'. We got out of the train. Of course, everyone laughed and pretended they'd known all along something of the sort would happen.

Next day we fell into our usual routine as though we had never been to the station. Certainly we cursed the Germans and cursed the British Government. (When we did get home, we learnt the hitch had been caused by the American Air Force hitting one of the hospital ships scheduled to take us from Germany.) Three days later we were again on our way, and this time slowly rolled north till we reached the coast and took ferry for Sweden. There we were to be exchanged for German prisoners. Three hundred of us passed through the gates on to the dock, a motley collection. I was the last to go, and I remember wondering if the gates might shut for some reason. Within a few hours we were entrained for Göteborg, passing our German opposite numbers *en route*, and there found three ships all emblazoned with the Red Cross. Ossie Younger and I shared a cabin on the *Drottningholm*, immediately dubbed the Trotting Home. After three and a half years, it seemed a certainty. Hills surround that harbour, and as we stood on deck in the dark our happiness was so great it seemed we were in fairyland. The

Swedes came out in thousands on those hills, and sang. And we sang back to them. I shall never forget that night. Late in the evening, Peggy and Victor Mallet, the British Minister to Sweden, came on board and sought me out, then Peggy went back to cable Victoria.

We sailed with every light ablaze and covered in Red Crosses, round the south and up the west coasts of Norway, until, on the second day, British planes from Scotland took us under escort, and early in the morning we edged slowly into Leith. Every siren was sounding, flags flying, and as the gangway lowered a band struck up. I cried quietly to myself. Life would be different now. No longer a soldier, I'd had it for that, anyway.

There was a reception party, photographers, bands, buns and tea. Unlimited ladies ready to do anything for the poor prisoners. For my part, like all the others, I was smart, clean, cheerful, but very moved and thoughtful. Although we'd been away for nearly four years it was quickly explained that we mustn't expect to go home yet. The Army Medical Authorities wished to examine us. We would all be sent to various hospitals. Highlanders longing to go north to the Highlands went south to Netley; I, longing to fly south to Victoria, went to Manchester. And so they shunted us, protesting but thankful to be home. Another reception at Manchester, and about midnight we sat down to a true British meal: roast beef, Yorkshire pudding and, of course, plum pudding. Apparently the medical authorities had forgotten that our prisoner years had left us with stomachs quite unable to do justice to it. But the meal meant nothing to me: all I wanted was to telephone my Victoria. That number could never leave my mind: Corsham 3270.

A rather sharp Hallo greeted me—Nanny not best pleased that a telephone ringing might have woken the dear little boys, Nicholas and Antony. Then *her* voice, after nearly four years. That night I slept well, oh, very well, though we knew we wouldn't get away the next day, when they subjected us every kind of probing and examination. But the following day surely? So my wrath can be imagined when the R.A.M.C. informed me (I was still the Senior Officer) that the War Office had regretfully decided we must stay on an extra day. The Press wished to interview us. Remonstrations were futile: it was the will, or shall I say wish, of the War Office.

I don't know whether the Press were disappointed or not, but during the night most men disappeared, and Ossie Younger, Antony de Salis and I left at crack of dawn for London.

How could I not remember that moment as the train drew into Euston Station?

PART TWO

17

We Build Again

War, fighting, a whole life gone west; but the link with everything worth living for was here. The engine gave those familiar last puffs, doors opened, and there stood Victoria. What can one possibly write or say of such moments? Time stopped and was our own for a while. I remember staying at the Meurice in what, so short a time before, would have seemed the incredibly remote luxury of a private suite. I remember a most perfect dinner which Victoria doubted I could eat but I did. Wisely she decided we would not go home next day but be alone together. We went to Harrods to see what could be found for Nicholas, and Antony whom I'd never seen. We bought them two wooden tanks. Before leaving in the morning I'd expected an enormous bill, when, much to my embarrassment, a note from the manager of the Meurice asked me to accept the visit with his compliments.

And so to Jaggards. We now had to plan a new life, for I had no intention of staying there: a 'stronghold of the Fullers'. Though I realised I was Miss Victoria Fuller's husband, and felt proud to be such, I knew a prolonged 'making a home within a home' would be a mistake. What could life be? I knew I would be 'boarded' out of the Army. Then what? I'd always wanted to grow flowers, and I wanted to be away with Victoria on our own as far as possible from other people. That, I'm sure, was a reaction from being cooped up and sleeping sardine-fashion for several years. I wanted to fling my arms, and feel nothing, to breathe and be free to walk where I wished. It happened after both Great Wars: many men returning wanted nothing but to get away from humanity, live in the country, to make and grow things. Only that had meaning.

We went north to Edinburgh to see the wives of officers and men of the Lothians. Not a happy or easy time, for many had lost their husbands or sons. Christmas came. I exerted myself, and Jaggards was superbly decorated. Nicholas enjoyed Father Christmas, Antony did not; neither did he like plum pudding. Then early in the New Year I received instructions to report to a board of doctors at Millbank.

At that time I had guiding vision, and with the help of a magnifying glass could read print out of the corner of one eye. Victoria and I were shown in to see Colonel King, a top eye specialist in civilian life, and an extremely nice and understanding person. After a long examination, he said candidly that no more operations could do any good: it was only a matter of time, possibly three or four years, before I would be completely blind. Looking back, I am very grateful to have been prepared in this way, but at the time I had great faith and was determined not to accept anything so final. However, they 'boarded' me, and within six months I would be retired on a one hundred per cent disability pension.

We left Millbank Hospital, a dreary place in war-time, and hurried off to Paddington with my railway warrant (at least I'd been given something), and handed it in at the R.T.O. Office, to be greeted by Major Arthur Bailey, who'd been at Weedon. He enquired who my attendant was—he didn't know Victoria—and, I suppose quite justifiably, she was rather angry at being called an attendant. Back at Jaggards we had time to think. Oddly enough, we weren't upset. At least we knew where we stood, we were together again, and I knew Victoria would see me through.

In March my D.S.O. was gazetted, and we went up to London for the investiture on June 19, the day after the Guards' Chapel was destroyed by a V-bomb. Victoria took the boys to Hamley's, and as they were walking down Regent Street everyone threw themselves on the pavement, except I think Nicholas, who went on rolling it with a toy roller. Antony was sick in the gutter, and all three arrived at the Cavalry Club with blackened faces. Another bomb had landed not far away. And then for a change we spent the afternoon at the Zoo, our fun often interrupted by further bombs. Next day we were told the investiture would not be held.

I wanted to grow flowers. Although I went to St Dunstan's, I couldn't rightly be accepted as a St Dunstaner because I still had sufficient sight to get around, but Sir Ian, later Lord Fraser gave me greater confidence and arranged that I should do a course of horticulture at Reading University. After four years apart, this was hardly to Victoria's liking, but as always in my life I simply would not do nothing, so from Monday to Friday I worked there and spent the week-ends at Jaggards. Now we began to look for a house. In order to have the 'early' market, I wanted to go to the West Country, so we searched Dorset and Somerset, which didn't seem to yield anything quite right, till by great good fortune Dee Hicks Beach told us a great friend of hers, Lady Poltimore, knew of just the house we wanted; it belonged to her son-in-law, Sir Dennis Stucley. A journey to Bideford was long in war-time. From Exeter we slowly rolled and halted, thirteen stops. Victoria complained it was farther than she ever wanted to go, and anyway it always rained in Devonshire, and she endeavoured to gain the support of a young R.A.F. pilot sitting opposite. Unfortunately he replied,

In actual fact, Chivenor is nearly always open for landing, there's never any fog.'

When the agent took us to see the house next morning, as Pillhead came in sight Victoria said, 'This is ours.' By September we'd settled into our home, this home which has provided so much happiness and, at times, despair. We had a gardener, Monty Burnett, who'd been at Pillhead since a boy; Mrs Cloak, who is still with me, came in each day; and soon there were two German prisoners of war to help. A greenhouse was built, laurels ripped up, the fence in front of the house moved back, rubbish cleared, and in no time the Pillhead Flower Farm was operating.

Then one day in December a telegram from Harry Faudell Phillips came, asking if I would allow my name to be proposed as Chairman of the British Show-Jumping Association. Horses had given me endless pleasure in my life, but I didn't intend to get involved again, I wanted to grow flowers. Victoria, though, knew me better, and wisely said, 'You can't stay here all the time and become a cabbage.' So I accepted, and in December 1944 was elected Chairman, that by one vote only. I could not possibly have guessed what it would entail and what it would come to mean.

At that time the B.S.J.A. had a membership of little over 500 and an income of about £500. But I quickly realised that this might be my opportunity to forward the plans I had mulled over and discussed when a prisoner. It seemed likely that hunting would gradually be curtailed because of its expense and by the spread of building; and that polo could not long continue on a pre-war scale, also on account of costs, and the lack of horsed soldiers to participate. I believed there would be a swing to what I term the more artificial horse sports. This swing has come, but not as fast as I then expected. There would be a great future for show-jumping, I was quite convinced of that, but several things had to be ensured: the enjoyment of the rider *and* the spectator, plus encouragement for the breeding and training of the best type of horse. I had plenty of time to think while I gardened.

On January 23 our daughter Sarah was born. A bitterly cold snap, and I sat up all night keeping the fires burning, and at the same time completed a book on the building of courses for show-jumping. This was the first book on the subject ever published, and although not very good soon sold out.

The garden grew, and so did my plans for show-jumping. There is a wood or bank at Pillhead full of snowdrops, and the selling of these was my first commercial enterprise. I picked and picked, and Victoria, sitting up in bed, bunched them. In the morning I pushed a bicycle into Bideford, where I either sold the snowdrops at eightpence a bunch, or sent them superbly packed to Covent Garden. At that time I was making my garden pay, and

I was determined that, although a sport, show-jumping must pay too, it must be self-supporting. The B.S.J.A. rented an office in Bedford Square, and I quickly discovered that since the secretary was not so enthusiastic as I, the simplest method of persuading him to resign would be to give him more and more work. That did the trick.

18

Flowers

Nineteen forty-five was to see the end of the War, but I'm not ashamed to say that for me it meant I now had a superb family—Nicholas, Antony and Sarah—and two great interests in life: I was determined to be a good gardener and, with the help of others, to make show-jumping a national sport of which this country could be proud. These two objectives might seem at odds with each other, but strangely they tied up. At home I was madly thinking of the family and the brightening of my 'cathedral', Pillhead, but while I quietly planted polyanthus I was wondering what should be done for show-jumping. I've been fortunate in having many friends to advise me, and my upbringing and training enabled me to decide whose advice to take. But for the moment let me cope with my garden.

Early in 1947, Mr Lee, my old Rough Riding Sergeant-Major, having left the Army and taken up a post with Vickers of Newcastle, decided he'd had enough and, whatever the pay, would prefer to work as an individual. He telephoned one morning and asked if he could come and work for me. Though delighted, I explained I couldn't pay him more than the agricultural wage—notoriously low—simply because I could not afford it. Later that day a telegram announced that he and his family had left and the furniture would follow later.

Now I believe, indeed know, that a market-gardener will never make money unless he either has a good deal of capital (which I did not) or is prepared to live in a caravan with his wife and family, working from early morning till dark. I wanted to succeed as a gardener and at the same time think out my responsibilities towards show-jumping. Even when I could see little and finally became blind, I always found plenty to do. Potting up plants was simple, and I had many a peaceful afternoon in the shed accompanied by my wireless set, listening to a Rugger International, Test Match or the Cup Final.

In recent years many afternoons have been spent clearing brambles and nettles. I put down a bleater and a line. The bleater pips away rather like a bell-buoy to give me my bearings, and armed with thick gloves and mackintosh trousers I set to on hands and knees. It kills two birds with one stone, because apart from clearing the ground I pour sweat and reduce weight.

When blind, quite soon one can tell whether a plant is in good condition or no by feeling the leaves: if they are shiny and soft, there is nothing wrong.

But to return to those early post-war years. I became convinced I had to specialise in something, and with the help of Archie Balfour of Sutton's I settled for two main projects: Devonshire being primrose country, polyanthus were the obvious things. But which? Blue were then in fashion, so blue it must be, and I've grown them for many years. Secondly, I'd become very interested in Gerberas, the Transvaal daisy: these beautiful plants have flowers of pastel colours and, though I suppose I shouldn't boast, are difficult to grow; the seed must be very fresh to obtain a good germination. Ian Fraser, who had interests in South Africa, got me seed of the Jamesonii hybrids. They certainly weren't easy but we soon had them flourishing and in 1947 decided to bring them to the fore. It seemed reasonable to exhibit at the Royal Horticultural Society Show in Vincent Square. But how? If we took up the plants, some of the blooms might be over before they were shown; so we brought up the blooms, all carefully packed with plenty of the dandelion type of leaves, and an ample supply of jam jars. We would 'mock up' an exhibit.

On arrival, I was shown to my stand by the secretary of the R.H.S., who enquired what I was going to exhibit the blooms *in*.

'Don't worry, I've brought plenty of jam jars,' I replied.

Said Mr Symonds, 'Jam jars are not used in the precincts of the Royal Horticultural Society.'

I'm afraid I brusquely countered with, 'These are special jam jars, and will be used.'

I'm glad to say that not only were the jam jars used, carefully covered with peat and moss, but we obtained a Certificate of Cultural Commendation. Great joy, for it is a considerable honour and our names even appeared in the *Daily Mirror*. Now on the horizon loomed the Chelsea Flower Show, and that really was an adventure. A mass of plants had to be grown, some in the greenhouse, some in the potting-shed to hold them back, and even some in the cellar at Pillhead to be in good company and really cool. The big day came and we exhibited our Gerberas in, I think, 1949. One of the glories of such an enterprise is finding how many friends one has—all the experts, Mr Allwood, Mr Hillier, Mr Waterer, helped us only too readily. Both H.M. Queen Mary and H.M. Queen Elizabeth (now the Queen Mother) came, and for three days Victoria and I stood explaining the virtues and vices of Gerberas. Sergeant-Major, or now Mr Lee was in his element: he explained to many a lady young or old that these plants were easy to grow, would indeed grow anywhere. One might venture, 'But my soil is very gravelly.' To which Mr Lee replied, 'Don't worry, madam. They will grow in your drive.' And another, overhearing, would say, 'Then will they overrun my herbaceous border?' At which Mr Lee would unhesitatingly fire, 'Madam, if that happens I will come down to thin them out for you!' Each evening at the Cavalry Club before dinner we delightedly added up our sales—and ordered a bottle of champagne. After four days, with our Silver Medal, we'd taken sufficient orders to buy a greenhouse to raise plants to be delivered the following year.

The garden grew, we sold more lettuces, started a Christmas gift scheme for gladioli, supplied Goodyear's of Brook Street with superb white delphiniums for fashionable weddings. We'd won a Silver Medal at the Chelsea Flower Show, but not far back in my mind the image flamed of a Gold Medal in the Olympics at Helsinki. These were the encouraging signs, both outward and self-induced. Previously in 1947, bending over a frame in the garden, my sight suddenly went once more: for no apparent reason the retina had torn again. I crept down to the house, and told Victoria I could see nothing. We sat in my study here, she as always full of reassurance.

At Moorfields Eye Hospital in London, Mr Davenport the St Dunstan's specialist came to give his verdict: another operation on my retinas—the seventh. He was not very optimistic, and when the bandages were removed there was little improvement. I could just tell the difference between night and day. I always remember Victoria trying me out. I was in bed and she was feeding me, and when the luncheon pudding came in I asked, 'What is it?' 'Something you love, darling.' I received a mouthful—blancmange! She'd caught me with the one thing I hated, and I spat it out.

I was now accepted as a St Dunstaner, and went to Avenue Road to do my training and be 'rehabilitated'. I had already learnt to type in Germany, and as for rehabilitation, that had been achieved the hard way, as a prisoner. However, St Dunstan's is a very great regiment and I always feel proud to belong to it. Lord and Lady Fraser have inspired us all to try and try like mad to be ordinary people and live useful lives. I learnt Braille, and at weekends carefully studied Aesop's *Fables* in the train. After five hours I knew why the crow had dropped a piece of cheese and who had caught it. In the week, the days were a routine, but that was easy for me: work in the morning, typewriting, Braille, then luncheon, and a walk in Regent's Park to feed the ducks. And as I moved round the lake, wondering vaguely if I might fall in, always I was thinking of how to put a sport, show-jumping, 'on the map'.

19

Show-Jumping—the New Look

During the winter of 1945, a hard one, I'd written that short book on the building of courses. Today it would be quite out of date, for then the distances between fences, the spreads and actual building of obstacles were imaginative but not sufficiently accurate. In my pre-war jumping days I'd walk round a course with some such expert as Dan Corry, we'd look at a combination of a double or treble of fences and quietly say, 'Well, that looks all right. Should ride with ease.' Within a few years I was to learn from riders like Harry Llewellyn, Pat Smythe and Peter Robeson how important it was really to measure and pace a distance, so that the rider could absolutely judge when to lengthen or shorten his horse's stride between these combinations.

As I saw it, the rider, the horse, the spectator must equally enjoy the competition, if show-jumping was really to be got going. The fences must encourage a horse to jump; consequently we'd get rid of flimsy obstacles which only forced the rider to check and not to ride confidently. Above all, we must have money to succeed, and that would only come if spectators enjoyed themselves and understood what was happening. Therefore the rules must be simple, with no room for the doubtful decisions we have in other games, the offside whistle to boos from the crowd, the foot fault shouted which unbalances the player. None of this would be easy to bring about, I knew. It was up to me to convince those on committees, *and* the riders.

Fortunately, I had Colonel Taffy Walwyn as President, Colonel V. D. S. Williams, Brigadier John Allen and Vera Allen on my first B.S.J.A. Committee. Then a letter from Lt-Colonel Harry Llewellyn in Brussels. Harry, whom I'd not met, came over and gave me great encouragement: apart from his knowledge, his enthusiasm was just what I needed. Perhaps (it's often been suggested) too many bloody colonels; but the one thing a good soldier understands is production. What can compare with the pre-war Tattoos, the present day Trooping of the Colour, the Mounting of Her Majesty's Guard? And those productions depend on the pride, discipline and readiness to obey of the soldier, so that training stood me in good stead in the years to come, when my friends and I organised the two London Horse Shows.

A suggestion to put on a one-day show at the White City, the Victory Championship for 1 September 1945, gave me my opportunity to have a go, trying out new ideas, although no rules had yet been changed. Henry Wynmalen designed some 'encouraging' fences: short wings and small shrubs enabled the spectator to see the poles clearly, the fences were brightly painted as an enticement to jump. At rehearsal on the Friday evening, one or two of my friends ran around knocking down fences so that the arena party could learn to re-erect them quickly. All went well. No detail overlooked. The Prize Money was good: First Prize £100. Jorrocks was the favourite. His owner, Joe Taylor, watched the rehearsal, looked at the fences, and finally came up to me and said 'You are daft. . . . Tom is not jumping my Jorrocks tomorrow!' I turned to Joe (later to become one of my greatest friends) saying, 'Oh dear, I am sorry. Nothing is going to be changed.' And walked away wondering if any of the others would say the same.

Next day my luck was in. Perfect weather, with an unexpected ten thousand spectators. All twenty horses started, including Jorrocks, who, alas, refused at the wall; after three-quarters of the competitors had completed, it looked as though Ted Williams on Umbo would be the winner, with half a fault from the fall of a slat (the abolition of that rule later on was to cause much controversy). Last to jump was my prisoner-of-war friend, Nat Kindersley, and all my thoughts were with him. He'd ridden his chestnut, Maguire, in the winning British team in London in 1939, and at the start of the war Mrs Kindersley had bought the horse out of the Army for £40. Fence after fence he cleared, until at the last, a formidable gate over five feet high, he almost stopped and in an unbelievable way corkscrewed over, landing on all fours. A delightful and dramatic end to my first big Show at the White City. Dorian Williams and Jack Webber were in the stands. I doubt if they guessed how we would all work together in the long years to come.

About this time Nicholas started at his preparatory school, Hawtrey's (St Michael's in my day), now in a lovely country house in the middle of Savernake Forest. Victoria disliked the idea of his going to boarding-school, and, when the day came for us to take him, was much more perturbed than master Nicholas. When we drove away, though he'd been told by the Headmaster to wave to Mummy and Daddy, Nicholas was too busy measuring the size of his foot against another new boy's. As soon as we were out of sight Victoria pulled up and fairly told me off. Why couldn't he go to day-school like other boys? Yet Nicholas did extremely well, as did Antony later; Nicholas becoming head boy and captaining the cricket eleven. I'm told he's like me in most ways: dislikes being beaten, although he doesn't show it. Even at home at Pillhead we made up a boys' eleven at times, and before they went to Instow to take on Admiral Sir Robin Durnford-Slater's boys' team, ours came to practise the day before. We left little to chance.

Nineteen forty-five certainly started us on the road to success in show-jumping. We'd proved a crowd could be raised to great excitement, I had complete confidence that all my plans floating on the distant horizon would not turn out to be a mirage. I've no doubt that enthusiasm overran itself sometimes. One of the best moves the B.S.J.A. ever made was to appoint Captain Jack Webber, late of Sam Browne's Indian Cavalry, as Secretary. I had the happiness of working with him for over twenty years, and he could always steady me. We then proceeded on Whyte Melville's principle when riding a horse: give an inch to take a mile.

I must for a moment digress, because something happened which seems to me a perfect intimation of what journalists and politicians call 'social change'. The equestrian sports are governed throughout the world by the *Fédération Equestre Internationale*. It was formed in the early twenties, with Commandant Hector as Secretary-General. Although Great Britain had been a member nation, we appeared never to send a representative to the General Assembly held each year in Paris. Victoria and I decided that I should go in 1946, particularly because of the forthcoming Olympics in two years' time.

Eighteen nations were represented, and we all sat around with President General Baron de Trannoy and Commandant Hector in a small room without even tables on which to write. The whole 'set-up' struck me as very amateurish and certainly inefficient. It was my first meeting, and consequently I sat quiet, except to propose that the definition of a 'Gentleman' be abolished. In the regulations a 'Gentleman' was defined as a rider of good breeding and high social standing. Amateurs and Professionals were carefully defined, and a rider might even be an 'Amateur Gentleman' or a 'Professional Gentleman'. Non-commissioned officers were not permitted to represent their country. It was not until some years later that I managed to get the definition of 'Gentleman' abolished, but on this occasion Monsieur Polyterniac asked me why I wished to get rid of this valuable distinction. '*Non*,' he said, 'I do not understand why you of all people should wish to abolish Gentlemen—after all, it is an English word!' I replied, 'It may be an English word, but there are none remaining.' He and the Bureau or Committee threw up their hands in horror and Commandant Hector rang his bell and passed on to the next item on the agenda.

At later meetings, with either Colonel Williams' or Ruby Holland-Martin's support, we did with difficulty force a vote.

It is interesting to me to look at my grandfather's commission from Her Majesty Queen Victoria: 'Richard Tuberville Ansell *esquire*, greeting.' Dated 1873. Again from Her Majesty, my father's: 'George Kirkpatrick Ansell, *gentleman*, greeting, 18 April 1894 to the 6th Dragoons.' Whereas I received my commission from H.M. King George V as 'to Michael Picton Ansell, greetings to the 5th/6th Dragoon Guards on 30 August 1924.' I was not described as either a gentleman or an esquire. Hardly surprising that I should wish to see this definition in the International Regulations removed.

After three days of meetings, Victoria and I went for a holiday to the South of France and stayed in a small hotel in Antibes. We were both so desperately happy. Saw the Nice flower markets again, and every morning walked miles around Antibes looking at the superb market gardens, the carnations, anemones and orchards full of mimosa. We even found a Dutchman growing large numbers of Gerberas: I learnt a lot from him. And I remember thinking how hard these small market growers had to work, and how tidy their gardens were.

At that time we were not supposed to take more than a very limited amount of currency out of this country: £25 I think. I knew Victoria would require an ample supply in Paris—deservedly so, for it was our first real holiday since before the war—and I had no guilty feelings as I hid the extra in the socks I was wearing. Victoria professed herself horrified, but having been searched many times in Germany I found it too easy to maintain an innocent look.

The B.S.J.A. had made a profit of £800 or so in 1945, and decided to repeat the one-day Show at the White City the following year. Though a financial failure, that was more than compensated for by the appearance of Lt-Colonel Harry Llewellyn. This brilliant horseman, equally in the hunting field, steeplechasing and the show-jumping arena, was exactly the kind of big star we badly needed in those early years. By an odd coincidence, after two clear rounds he tied with Douglas Bunn, then only eighteen: these two between them were to influence show-jumping so much in the next twenty years.

Now in 1946 began the long battle to get rules changed. I had a superb committee to help me, some were 'difficult', and just as well at times, for I then had to go slowly to convince them. If we were ever to be good enough to compete with and beat our friends from overseas, our riders had to gain experience under International Rules. Under our *National* Rules, light flimsy slats were placed on the top of each fence: if knocked off that cost the rider a half fault. Knocking down a fence with the forelegs scored four faults, but only two faults with the hind legs, and one fault for each foot in the water. Time played little part, riders even being permitted to circle or halt before jumping the water while the martingale was undone.

Judges' decisions were often questioned, therefore: had the slat been blown off by the wind, or was it the horse's tail? Had the fence been knocked down by the horse's fore or hind legs or even his belly? And so on and so on. I knew changes would only come slowly, because some of my own friends had trained their horses for winning under those National Rules and one couldn't immediately convince them they would ultimately be successful under the more streamlined International code. Oddly, it was even more difficult to persuade them that the public actually *wanted* a winning British Team and would then flock to see them. In consequence there'd be greater prize money and horses could only become more valuable. Everyone would benefit. I was so sure, that I wrote to my old pal Dan Corry telling him to buy every good jumper he could lay hands on—I would make him a fortune. He still has that letter.

Jack Webber and I realised what we had taken on. Together we toured the countryside attending meeting after meeting. From Doncaster to Chester to Warwick, we circled around, usually, like any politician, dogged by hecklers good-natured in this case—such as Phil Oliver, Edgar, Lane and others. Each successive night they threw the same questions at me, so, like those politicians, I always had the answers ready.

Had I anticipated the extent of the row that blew up, I might not have let myself be drawn back into the horse world. (On my return from Germany Victoria had thought I should become a politician or a priest. I fear I said, 'No, thank you. Too many hypocrites.') After one Annual General Meeting, going down in the lift, one of our members told me he was off to his solicitors to take out an injunction against my changing *any other rules*. But it was rare for anything to be put to the vote. We could agree. Jack Webber used to spare me hours, the night before a meeting, doing our homework. Such great stalwarts of the old school as Joe Taylor, Andrew Massarella, Wilf White, Frank Allison then did battle with the perhaps more forward-looking Harry Llewellyn, John Allen, Phil Blackmore or Michael Ansell disguised. Having given way, poor Joe Taylor travelled back to Lancashire convinced he had made a mistake, to endure a sleepless night thinking of how he had been conned, till finally he would ring me up in the dead hours.

Nearly every week I flogged up by train from Bideford the five or six hours to Waterloo or Paddington. I must have got to know nearly every porter and ticket collector, and many of the engine drivers. I enjoyed talking to them, and of course in later years, because of television, they would tell me how stupid Harry or Pat had been to hit the wall or whatever, or how wonderful that they'd won. I've had many a happy journey in the driver's cab from Taunton to Barnstaple, or Barnstaple to Exeter, with my pal George Capel, not only a senior engine driver but a J.P. and member of the Rural District Council. The night journeys were particularly long and tedious. I still spent my time thinking and knitting, but didn't have the day-time amusement of sitting in a carriage full of big businessmen reading their *Times* or perhaps the *Financial Times*. I could feel them slowly lower their papers and stare at that half-witted man knitting. Always I carried two sleeves, or a back and a front, for fear I'd drop a stitch and there'd be no one capable of picking it up. Once, on the way to Exeter, there wasn't enough elbow room, so I moved to a non-smoker. Soon I became instinctively aware that someone opposite was watching me. I went on knitting, and then a hesitant voice enquired, 'It's not Colonel Ansell, is it?' I recognised the voice: Gordon Richards. He'd often been to the London shows, and we knew each other well, but he didn't believe I knitted.

With the Olympic Games to be held in London in 1948 it was vital for our riders to gain experience, and that meant going abroad. Where was the money to come from? At a meeting at 66 Sloane Street I emphasised we must send a team to Nice and Rome and 'What about the cash?' We were fortunate in having such men as Cecil Murray and Bob Hanson in the early days (and Bob Dean and Bill Barton, a little later), all business men who understood the meaning of success. Within a few minutes at that meeting I had £200 on the table, and that was the beginning of the Olympic Games and International Equestrian Fund.

So in May 1947 the first British Show-Jumping Team made up of civilian riders travelled to Nice and Rome. Victoria and I fully intended going to Nice, partly for nostalgic reasons (I'd done well there in 1939), but my sight went again, this time more or less for good, and I ended up in Moorfields Hospital. The team learned much—above all, how much we had to learn—and Harry returned full of enthusiasm after a fine win on Kilgeddin in the Rome 'Puissance'.

The International Horse Show was revived that year. Many regretted the departure from Olympia, but the White City provided a perfect setting. Two things stand out: the winner of the Daily Mail Cup, Brian Butler, on his pale chestnut horse Tankard—everything flying (as it was described to me)—mane, tail, long black hunting coat: a brilliant win, with the only clear round; and, of course, the advent of *the* combination of this century, Foxhunter, ridden by Harry Llewellyn.

Nineteen forty-eight loomed, and how thankful I was when Geoffrey Cross, for so long Chairman of the Royal Windsor Horse Show, and I were both able to explain, at a council meeting of the British Horse Society, our horror at the proposal that Great Britain should *not* compete in the forthcoming Three-Day Event of the Olympics. We are, surely, a nation of horsemen and horsewomen. I don't know whether it was a symptom of postwar dispiritedness, but happily Geoffrey Cross helped me—and I'm glad to look back on it—to persuade the Council that entry was a MUST.

20

◆◆◆

1948—Bronze

The Olympic Games were to be held in London, and the Show-Jumping, as always on the last day, would be in the Wembley Stadium. I was in the happy but not entirely enviable position of being chairman of the selection committee and also responsible for designing and laying out the course. Naturally that gave me great 'scope', but I was strictly honest. A friend had made me a mass of small model fences all to scale, and these were magnetised and would stick to my metal Wembley Arena wherever I placed them. Not an easy job, for I had nothing like the knowledge of the present-day course builder, but I did it, and Mr Rodwell of Hampshire built the fences at his home: no one was to see them.

I could now return more regularly to Bideford, getting used to my nearly vanished sight. In the garden it mattered little: I knew every part and Victoria wisely let me get on with it. We took great pride in our bunching and packing. Nothing but the best we could produce was put on the train for either Goodyear's or Poupart's in Covent Garden. Naturally the constant worry was what would we get for the narcissus, polyanthus or freesias? I would telephone my friend Mr Hobbs in the morning, at Covent Garden: 'What are Carlton daffodils making?' The answer might be 'two shillings a bunch'. Then we'd pick and pick, bunching on a rack holding three or four in a line, while Mr Lee collected foliage from the naturalised narcissus in the 'wilderness' or wild garden. How exciting to hear they'd made three shillings a bunch—and woe when the price had dropped; and worse when an invoice was returned marked 'no sale'. Growing cut flowers can be hell: it's an extraordinary thing how at week-ends all the narcissi, gladioli or Iceland poppies seem to come ready for picking—so Saturday and Sunday become the busy days. But that gave me many hours to brood over the Olympics.

We took a team of possibles to compete at Lucerne, where Victoria and I had a lovely room high up overlooking the lake, and here each morning, after an early breakfast of rolls, coffee and that incomparable cherry jam, I went off to see Colonel Haccius. I still think him the best designer of courses I've ever known, and he taught me how an expert can arrange the distances

112

between fences to help a particular type of horse or rider. The Show ran on during ten days in what we might call a leisurely fashion, which would hardly be acceptable in our busy London. Wonderful days of rest, cruising around the lake or walking the mountains—where we found gentians and the first narcissi as the snow crept back.

After a final trial at the White City, our team was selected, and the lOympic Three-Day Event took place at Aldershot. Although we weren't successful, the Duke of Beaufort was inspired by the competition, and his encouragement and generosity have had an immeasurable influence on our triumphs over—well, it's incredible to think that it is nearly a quarter of a century. Two slightly disastrous incidents occurred. As so often, the judges disagreed in the Dressage but eventually a Swede was declared a medallist: he appeared rather an elderly gentleman to be a second lieutenant in the Swedish Army, and I said to Jack Webber, 'Promotion there must be slow.' As I've already mentioned, non-commissioned officers were still not allowed to compete in the Games, and the Army authorities in Sweden had seen fit to promote this rider; but immediately on his return, Army orders announced his reversion to warrant officer. Unfortunately, these orders were sent to all Military Attachés, and the French one made a considerable fuss when he learnt of the demotion: as a French officer had been next in the Dressage placings, he finally got the medal. The other incident lacked this hilarious element. The Danish team was leading in the Three-Day Event, and on the show-jumping day they examined and walked the course carefully; a correction was announced which the Danish rider didn't hear, and he took the wrong course, thus eliminating his team. Personally, I have never changed any condition unless sure that every competitor knew of it: one shouldn't have to learn a lesson so dearly.

The final day at Wembley, my responsibility, loomed. Heavy rain and footballers between them had churned up the ground to what in Devon we would call a 'prahpurr' mess, when I took it over at nine-thirty on the Friday night; and we then had to build a course of fifteen heavy fences, dig four ditches and a water-jump. (No complaint from the riders next day. Rather a different story twenty-one years later when our footballers complained because horses had left hoof-marks on 'their' Wembley turf.) Impossible to use tractors, so every fence and barrow-full of sand had to be manhandled on to the turf or rather mud. By about 3.00 a.m. ditches had been dug, lined and revetted, and everything was in position. We all 'fell out' and went to a canteen to drink tea and eat pork pies. I was amazed the work had been done that quickly, and said so to George Stanton, then chief engineer: he explained that he estimated how long it would take and would pay them on that basis; he thought they'd need till 6.00 a.m., but now they could go home and still be paid till that hour. That principle should be made law.

We quietly checked everything and then dossed down on some camp-beds to wait for morning. The Olympic flame just flickering.

When a vast crowd of eighty thousand opened up with community singing, on that most glorious hot sunny day, the colouring of the ladies' dresses, the national flags and the flowers were something I could only imagine as perfection. Could Great Britain make a real start on the long road to success? The Duke of Beaufort, President of the Jury, sat with hands clasped over the bell. (The French co-judge, over excited, had a tendency to bounce up and down shrieking '*Sonnez! Sonnez!*'—and lunge towards it.) Jack Webber, George Stanton, Phil Blackmore and I sat on the running track watching the water level in the ditches: we feared they were leaking. They were. At regular intervals we received telephone calls from the President of the Jury to 'fill up those water fences'. Eventually, on the advice of George Stanton, I replied that the London Water Board had turned off the water. Anyway, it was the same for all.

It was a difficult course, and when Major Umberto Marilès Cortez, later to become General, started on his final round, the last to jump, he had everything against him: the going badly poached, the water level still sinking, and knowing he could afford no more than seven faults to win a Gold Medal for the Individual *and* the Mexican Team. Though slow, he was clear to the water and the final wall when, in a tense silence, he pulled down to a canter, deliberately jumped into the water to give away four faults, then pushed on for the wall, which he jumped with ease. No one else in the world at that time would have taken such a risk, but he was a great rider, and competitions are won by those who take risks. Mexico took the Gold, Spain the Silver and Great Britain won the Bronze, her first Olympic Medal in Show-Jumping. We had made our start. And I know mine were not the only thanks that went up into the sky when a choir conducted by Sir Malcolm Sargent sang the Olympic Hymn. It is always a moving occasion, and we can never forget that in Ancient Greece a citizen would leave everything, even if he were engaged in warfare, to compete at Olympia. Why has that lesson not been learnt?

On the following Tuesday we'd moved to the White City for the International Horse Show. This was no anticlimax, for with that Bronze Medal our blood was up, and against very strong opposition from Spain, France, Italy, Sweden, Turkey and the United States (who incidentally had not done well in the Olympic Games, with a fine team), we took the King's Cup, that most coveted trophy in the world. Already I'd learnt that spectators don't enjoy a competition meandering on for hours; it was much better to break down a large class into sections, allowing so many through to the final. Competitors prefer it too. A good example of what we wanted to avoid occurred at Zürich in 1949: jumping started at two o'clock in the afternoon, and by one the following morning, without a break, the second class had been completed. There was an indoor show, with various trade stands, at one of which hunting clothes were exhibited: wax models in breeches, red coat, etc. Victoria, Wilf White and I stopped to look at this, and suddenly realised Harry Llewellyn was seated among the wax dummies. Half asleep, he'd decided he might just as well exhibit himself there as watch the interminable dreary rounds. Small wonder the Zürich Show packed up later for lack of support.

Nineteen forty-eight was the first and last occasion on which lady riders were allowed to compete in the King George V Cup—among the finalists, Pat Smythe, then nineteen, and Lulu Rochford. Harry Llewellyn won on Foxhunter in inimitable fashion, and his victory, coming on top of the Olympic medal, gave show-jumping wonderful publicity. Occasionally in later years at the Horse of the Year Show, I'm afraid I used to paste up the posters 'Foxhunter jumps tonight'. Harry wasn't over-pleased at that, but he accepted it philosophically, we remained close friends, and the show benefited. Now our field-glasses were lifted towards Helsinki, four years away. There must be Gold in the far north.

This year was, I believe, the beginning of an era, when we in this country began to understand the meaning of success in international sport. I'd been fortunate in gaining the confidence of some of the die-hards of the old British Show-Jumping Association. The Duke of Beaufort encouraged us by offering Badminton as the venue for a future three-day event. Badminton started in 1949 and grew until it is now the finest event of its kind in the world. Colonel Williams and I travelled to Paris to see an indoor Show, *Le Jumping*: the arena very small, but the crowd and the enthusiasm unbelievable. I came back convinced that if France could promote a Show of such calibre we could certainly do better. Tony Collings, the owner of the Porlock Vale Riding School, was an immense enthusiast, and he suggested to the British Horse Society that they should promote an indoor Show late in the season. It would be known as 'The Horse of the Year Show'.

21

Horse of the Year Show

Following Tony Collings' ideas, I set about planning a Horse of the Year Show in January 1949. We plotted the schedule, and with the help of a large picture of the Harringay arena even designed the poster. Tony didn't mind that I've always found it better, once one has an idea, to work through the night and so avoid telephone calls. Our most pressing problem was, who would pay the loss if there were a loss? Mr Frank Gentle and the Greyhound Racing Association agreed to cover it for the first year, provided they had an option for the following year. A committee was essential, and it couldn't just be composed of my friends in the B.S.J.A.: all elements in the horse world would have to be represented. We could reasonably assume that it would take a couple of years to get the thing off the ground—for I never thought it would fail.

The show opened on 13 September 1949, running for three days. We had splendid riders from France: d'Orgeix, d'Oriola and Michèle Cancre; the Belgian, Charles de Selliers, with his great horse Sea Prince, and all our rising stars at home backed me. Jack Webber and I travelled daily to and from Harringay by underground, no money in the till to pay expenses. We came to know Mansion House tube station well. On the night before the opening we'd had a rehearsal when everything conceivable seemed to go wrong. We couldn't afford a band and had engaged a well-known player of harmoniums or organs—he arrived to find his organ was presumably somewhere on the way from Blackpool; when Harry Llewellyn came in to have a quiet look at the course it had turned up and was in full bellow, so he rounded on me saying, 'Have I come to the wrong place, is this the "400"?' Walking to the station late that night, Tony coolly assured me that a bad rehearsal always meant a good Show, but when I got to my room at the Cavalry Club I could not agree with him: I'd lost all the course plans—in the Underground, I presumed. (Next morning it turned out that Major David Satow, one of my stewards, had taken them home in his car: one's very unlucky to have two bad days running.)

On the Monday before the opening Jack Webber and I had stood in a steady drizzle watching the Box Office. It was a night of Greyhound Racing.

Every quarter of an hour someone would drop in to book a ticket for this new show, The Horse of the Year. We opened with £69 in the till.

The show ran its three days, and fortunately became a duel between Harry Llewellyn and d'Orgeix and Michèle Cancre (later to marry d'Orgeix). But what really won the day was Pat Smythe taking the supreme championship on Finality. I learned I'd been too ambitious: a mistake to believe that three separate courses could be built without endless delays. We all worked desperately hard, but deservedly received the slow hand-clap as Phil Blackmore and I bustled around measuring fences which had been slowly wheeled in on trucks used for the Harringay Circus. I vowed never again to wear a dinner jacket at a show: too conspicuous. It took twenty minutes to build a course, so in order to start the evening session with jumping it obviously had to be built during the interval between afternoon and evening programmes. At the end of the competition the centre had to be cleared and awards given, then I had to put on the reverse of a 'front cloth' scene in the theatre (while furniture and scenery were moved behind): we had a spotlight act in the centre while the perimeter was being rearranged. In 1931, competing at Toronto, I'd watched their ice hockey. During the interval the ice was swept by an arena party on skates and as a drill—why shouldn't we do the same, using heavy horses, Shires, Percherons, Suffolks and Clydesdales, to harrow the arena? Barry Pride, one of the senior stewards who had helped me throughout, composed the figures of this 'Heavy Horse Drive' and even got Sir Malcolm Sargent to advise on the music. We then devised another centre 'front cloth' scene for use while the outside fences were going up for the second and major jumping competition: the parade of the 'Personalities'.

On the last night of that opening Show the enthusiasm was wonderful, and I knew the battle had already been won—much of it thanks to Pat Smythe and Finality. One of my greatest blessings in life is that on many occasions the horse I've wanted to win, has won.

The loss was £2,400, which the Greyhound Association underwrote, asking me to do better next year. In 1950 we *were* better organised, and the show I've outlined above took shape; Phil Blackmore and I didn't wear dinner jackets, and there was no slow hand-clap. On Saturday night we had the first great thrill of putting up 'House Full' notices. Victoria and I could now stay at the Hyde Park Hotel, and let the Show pay for a car to and from Harringay.

Although the loss had been reduced to £800, the G.R.A. decided we could continue with the Show but must stand on our own feet: i.e. pay the rent and all the costs. I knew I couldn't expect the B.S.J.A. to accept this, so I asked a great number of generous people (whom I cannot name) and in no time had twenty to guarantee the loss. They demanded nothing in return but a Silver Badge. The cost of putting on the Show in those early days was about £10,500, and we very soon showed a profit of 20 per cent. Today it costs nearly £75,000, and yet we still maintain our profit at 20 per cent. All this money has been ploughed back into the sport of show-jumping, and no individuals have benefited.

In 1951 we learned a hideous lesson. The laying of a floor in an indoor arena always creates problems, and that year the soil, 800 tons of it, was brought under cover a week before the opening. On the eve of laying it there was a flood; rain poured down, drains were blocked, and although under cover the soil became sodden. Our contractors laid the floor, but when David Satow and I came down a day or two before 'take off' we could hardly walk across without gumboots. David and I stayed through most of the following nights while the soil was forked and sawdust added. Talk about a heavy plough in Essex.

Jumping started in the morning, and by four o'clock in the afternoon there hadn't been a single clear round. I was in despair, spending a penny in the gents, when I suddenly heard loud applause. Dawn Palethorpe had come to my rescue, the ground had begun to break up and she, with Earlsrath Rambler, had jumped the first clear round. But the arena looked a real mess, and the stewards worked even longer hours than usual those following days.

Their Royal Highnesses Princess Elizabeth and Prince Philip joined us on the Thursday, and luckily we had a grand duel between Harry Llewellyn and d'Orgeix. Harry, I'm glad to say, won. It fascinated me to learn that Prince Philip used opera-glasses and obviously *missed nothing*. I realised how characteristic it was of him when Prince Philip later became President of the British Horse Society, and also of the *Fédération Equestre Internationale*. Despite the floor, we won through that year, 1951, and showed a profit of £2,400.

I was born under Aries, which they tell me is appropriate for a soldier, and by this time had learned how to build up a team of officials and stewards: I proudly think them second to none. Dorian Williams is a splendid commentator, and, even more important to me, knows much about production and music; John Blackmore, the most conscientious of all secretaries; David Satow and Phil Blackmore in the ring; and General Vivian Street, a highly trained staff officer to steer me around and do my work. We all worked as a team, and each morning at twelve o'clock had a conference at which we went through every detail. We still do. It's obviously impossible to name every person in that team, but suffice to say that, as a team, everything that was asked was done.

We had many a famous horse in the Parade of Personalities. Tosca and her foal, Foxhunter, E.S.B., the Grand National winner, and Her Majesty Queen Elizabeth the Queen Mother's Devon Loch, ridden by Dick Francis. And even Hyperion, greatest of all stallions, who unfortunately believed the arena was his mating box. 'Dim the lights,' Dorian would say, and Hyperion would leave rather despondent.

In 1951 I was asked to manage both the Horse of the Year Show and the International Horse Show with the same staff. A staff of three, John, Jean and Marigold, worked in the basement of 66 Sloane Street, and with the help of David Satow the enterprise seemed to blossom. In my very first year with the International, I removed the deficit of £4,500 and turned it into the black where it has remained ever since. The major task being to make the two events different, in early years my problem was simplified: out of doors on warm sunny days the International became almost a fashion parade, whereas the other, in a small arena, I might term a 'Horse Revue'. Indoors the public are so close one cannot afford any mistake: timing must be perfection.

Being blind I have the advantage I'm always thinking ahead, and always have my finger on my watch. Usually I stand by 'Control' and dislike it intensely if anyone comes and speaks to me. In fact one nice person was told rather bluntly to go away, at which he succinctly said, 'I realise that your ears at a Show are my eyes.'

We've always been concerned to ring the changes on entertainments other than jumping at the Horse of the Year Show. Pageants are satisfactory, though things like the 'Midnight Steeplechase' need a lot of rehearsal and cost much. So in 1965 I was delighted when, at Badminton, Prince Philip told me that he was tired of watching 'the young trotting and cantering around the ring on their Show ponies and obviously getting into trouble from the parents if they did not win'. Surely I could arrange races for them, make it more exciting and the ponies needn't necessarily be 'Show' ponies. I was delighted: that was just what we wanted. Colonel Guy Cubitt encouraged us, and with Charles Adderley and Raymond Brooks-Ward's help we set about preparing Games: these were always for teams of four, no prize money, only rosettes. I sent my suggestions to His Royal Highness, and wasn't in the least surprised to receive a letter containing many amendments and improvements. The Prince Philip Mounted Games came into being in 1959 and the following year were really on the map; now any number of teams up to about one hundred and eighty enter. The idea of these Games was the first of many Prince Philip has passed on to me to try and use. They've now spread to Canada and America, and from 1972 have been included in the F.E.I. list of International Rules.

Her Majesty the Queen and Prince Philip again visited the Show in 1958. Whenever the Queen or, for that matter, any member of the Royal Family is present it puts us all on our toes: we want nothing but the best. On that night at Harringay Mrs Boon, a great rider, had a bad fall. The doctor and stretcher party were quickly in the arena (we rehearse all these things), lights dimmed and the band of the Royal Corps of Transport played lively music. Mrs Boon was carried out, and almost immediately Dorian Williams was able to announce that she wasn't seriously hurt. Later that night the Duke and Duchess of Norfolk invited Victoria and myself to supper at Claridge's. Almost as soon as I arrived Prince Philip asked me, 'Why did the band have to play such lively music for that poor girl on the stretcher?' I replied, 'I can only suppose, sir, that we should have played "Wrap me up in my tarpaulin jacket".'

At supper I had the honour of sitting next to Her Majesty. Either grouse or partridge was served, and the Queen took my plate, quietly saying with a laugh, 'Mike, I am used to doing this. I was doing it for my corgis at luncheon.' The plate was returned with everything perfectly cut up.

After ten years there, Harringay had to be sold and our only alternatives now were Earls Court, Olympia or the Empire Pool at Wembley. Thank heaven it turned out to be the last. The Chairman of Wembley at that time was Sir John Bracewell Smith, a Yorkshireman. I found it so very easy to agree terms with him: I knew what we could afford, he knew what was fair, and everything would be agreed in two or three minutes over a cup of tea. All those working at Wembley were on our side, and as the years have gone by the Shows have become famous for their clockwork precision—of which I always like to boast a little. A well-known Canadian businessman, Mr E. P. Taylor, dining one day with Bob Hanson, turned to him and said, 'The great thing about your two London Shows is that I never need look at my watch—all I have to do is look at the timings on your programme.' But clockwork precision or no, we had our fun behind the scenes.

For my highly efficient team of stewards the hours of the Show were long, often starting at seven in the morning and not finishing until late the same night or even early the next morning. Yet to those in the stands they never appeared tired, and we only kept going because we all had that essential part of our character, a sense of humour, and endless was the 'leg-pulling'. David Satow, the leader of all 'leg-pullers' would be sent to straighten a flag in the roof, and although he hated that cat-walk he went. There was always the fear from George Stanton that we might damage his freezing pipes for the ice in the floor. Eventually George gave up complaining about his pipes after I decided to settle it once and for all and really make him think. During our serious noon conference the smart Warrant Officer from the Arena Party entered and the conversation went as follows: 'Colonel.' Reply: 'Wait. Can't you see we are in conference?' 'But, Colonel.' Again from me: 'Wait.' 'Please, Colonel. Colonel Talbot-Ponsonby says the floor at one end of the arena is becoming very soggy.' That was sufficient. Without a word the white-faced George Stanton, and Jack Webber, just left, to return five minutes later to say, 'You b——.' I didn't always get things my way, though, for one day when walking back after a rehearsal of Cavalcade for the final night, on leaving the arena to change I was almost floored by a shower of skins: goat skins, sheep skins and any odd skin came down from those posted in the roof. This was a physical pun on my regiment, the Inniskillings, sometimes referred to as the 'Skins'. George Stanton certainly won that one, and Wembley Stadium paid the bill. Without this humour behind the scenes we could not keep going.

It would be easy to write a book on the Horse of the Year Show. The atmosphere is so very happy. Many gain great distinction, but none more deserving than my stewards, who work long hours without question, and for next to nothing, because they want to. The Band under Captain Desmond Walker, the Arena party, the Wembley Staff: they make one tremendous team. The stewards are all my friends, and my problem has been keeping the numbers down. My sons worked in the arena building courses, my daughter Sarah was a 'rosette' girl, an award steward for many years. And Victoria was ever there, helping, entertaining, encouraging when things went wrong.

When Her Royal Highness Princess Anne cut the twenty-first birthday cake on 11 October 1969, the British Show-Jumping Association and charities had received over £200,000 from the Horse of the Year Show Committee. For every night is now a sell-out, and the touts are standing outside selling any tickets they can get: when that happens you're really 'in business'.

I've often been asked what I remember as the greatest moment of these performances. Each year I incline to think, 'Well, this year has been our best,' but, looking back, I think the picture that touches my imagination most is of Anne, Duchess of Westminster, in 1969, allowing Arkle to join the Parade of Personalities. He was so proud, they told me, head held high, he looked around when he entered as if he owned Wembley. He certainly owned the love of the spectators, and each evening as the Duchess went out to give him a lump of sugar, he quite rightly bowed to her, and to the tumultuous applause.

By tradition the show closes with the Cavalcade. Horse or pony, one after the other, they take up their positions until over one hundred and fifty have patterned the arena, and in the place of honour under the centre lights stand the 'great' horses of the year with their riders. Maybe the Gold Medal Three-Day Event Team. Maybe David Broome, the World Show-Jumping Champion. Perhaps Mary Gordon Watson on Cornishman, and, of course, Arkle with Pat Taaffe. But how wonderful it was in 1971, when Her Royal Highness Princess Anne and Ann Moore stood together as European Champions.

Twenty years ago, travelling to Devon with my friend Ronald Duncan, I told him of this Cavalcade and asked him to write me a tribute to the

Horse. He did it during the journey, and each year the Show is brought to a close by the reading of this Tribute:

> This Cavalcade of Grace now stands, it speaks
> in silence, its story is this land.
>
> Where in this wide world can man find nobility
> without pride, friendship without envy or
> beauty without vanity? Here, where grace is
> laced with muscle, and strength by gentleness
> confined.
>
> He serves without servility; he has fought
> without enmity. There is nothing so powerful,
> nothing less violent; there is nothing so
> quick, nothing more patient.
>
> England's past has been borne on his back.
> All our history is his industry: we are his
> heirs, he our inheritance.
>
> Ladies and Gentlemen: THE HORSE!

22

✦✦

Final Acceptance

I was now forty-four years old and had to accept that I would be blind for good. Of course, I knew it; I'd been told so; but up to then some part of my mind had refused to absorb the fact, to acquiesce. My eternal optimism, I suppose. Fortunately my working life was clear. I knew what I wanted to do in the horse world, at home in the garden I knew every tree, stone and plant, and with Victoria's encouragement I felt our growing family would turn out well. Of course, blindness makes for a very lonely life at times, particularly travelling, but I never forgot Lord Fraser's belief that we could still do many things as well, and occasionally even better, than a sighted person. Victoria and I attended some of the St Dunstan's reunions, and I admit the mere fact of meeting others even worse off gave me the urge to try and do better. St Dunstaners succeeded almost unbelievably well as telephonists, at secretarial work, with machine tools, at pig farming, at poultry farming and, naturally, physiotherapy.

You have accepted your fate when you can say without embarrassment to people, 'I'm blind. Would you please help me.' Travelling by air was simple. I had to go a good deal to Paris, Geneva and Brussels for meetings and often went alone because of the expense. On arrival at London Airport, V.I.P. treatment: a charming air hostess swept me through the Customs to the plane. Once flying to Brussels I had an even more attentive charmer, for on landing she offered to take me in the underground to the Air Terminal, then insisted on seeing I arrived safely at the hotel—by the time we came to the reception desk I was beginning to wonder how much farther I'd be taken.

This travelling alone may be all right, but the unpacking is not so easy. What do I wear tomorrow? I have learned to put a matchstick in the pocket of my 'day' suits, and suitable ties have a knot. One's trouble is to ensure that the suit with the matchstick has the right pair of trousers. Not always correct, as on one occasion in the Cavalry Club Jack Webber very quietly told me my trousers did not go with my coat.

In Devonshire at this time walking was easy; there were few cars on our lanes, these bounded by high banks and hedges so one could not leave the road. I had three regular routes, one of about three miles, another of five

123

and a third of about nine. Using a long thumb-stick I rarely had trouble Only if a gale was blowing was I bothered: as already noted, my ears are often my eyes. I soon learned to recognise where I might be—for instance by the echo of my boots sounding back from a barn or cottage; but, of course, a carpet of snow would spoil that. Occasionally I walked into a parked car, and I remember Victoria's horror when I once returned with a black eye and bleeding nose. I think my reaction used to be 'how stupid' rather than 'what bad luck'. One day in London I tried to cross a road and bumped into a motor-cycle without harm to the rider or myself. In the same charmed way, arriving to get my hair cut I walked through a plate-glass door (I'd never known it shut before): no harm except to the door, for the rim of my bowler had protected me.

Most important, my life was desperately full in these three years, 1949-51, and that doubtless helped me through this final 'change-over'.

After the first Three-Day Event at Badminton in 1949 the whole of the 'Horse World' seemed to grow fast. A great friend of pre-war days, Colonel Trevor Horn, built up Badminton, and he wanted it not to become too large and 'commercialised': a national hunt meeting at Cheltenham, so to speak, rather than Derby Day at Epsom. But once again 'social change' could not be defied and the success story of the Three-Day Event riders would not permit this sport to remain static. Trevor was ably assisted by Colonel Gordon Cox-Cox and Colonel Babe Moseley—one more take-over by 'the colonels'! The Duke and Duchess of Beaufort gave every encouragement, though surely at times 'Master' must have looked out in despair at his lovely park, after the event had ended. Her Grace always asked us to stay, and for many years we had the same rooms: they'd once been Master's schoolrooms. What great fun we all had, but unfortunately the schoolroom was about as far away as it's possible to imagine. There'd be a sudden rush to change for dinner, and then quickly (but not too quickly) down endless and polished stairs.

Even the 'horse' world at Pillhead grew. The local Torrington farmers and Stevenston Pony Club had rallies in our front field, when Mr Lee used to instruct. As I'd hoped, all three children were enthusiastic about riding, particularly Nicholas; and there were the big days when all of them returned with ponies covered in rosettes from gymkhana events.

Both boys went to Wellington, and never seemed to have worries about passing examinations: the great thing about Hawtrey's, in their time, being that they were taught to enjoy academic work—very different from my day. My poor Sarah was not so lucky; and I remember a particular letter. Victoria being away, I asked Sarah to read it, and in a minute was appalled to hear her sobbing. In between snuffles she read a 'communication' from the Head Mistress at St Mary's, Wantage, telling me they could not accept Sarah as her standard of work was so low. In something like a fury I replied to this lady, suggesting that she think again, otherwise it would be St Mary's loss, not Sarah's. They did think again, and I turned out to be right, for my daughter did extremely well there: proof perhaps of how haphazard educational decisions can be. Victoria was in the West Indies when this happened, and, incidentally, it was also when I wrote the first part of this book: occupation being the best cure for loneliness.

The Helsinki Olympics were now our goal, and it was imperative that our riders got as much international experience as possible: useless to be sitting in our own back gardens thinking how good we were. Essential to compete in America and Canada as well as Europe. Even more important, no good just training five riders and sticking to that same team year after year: the unwisdom of that has been proved time and again—conspicuously in Ireland where, in pre-war days, Fred Ahearn, Dan Corry, Jed O'Dwyer, Jim Lewis and Cyril Harty were wellnigh unbeatable. Sadly, since that group broke up in 1948 no really good Irish Team has appeared. During the years 1949–52 we built up a wide base of riders and that base has continued to widen throughout the last twenty years. To do it the Association had to have money. Sending a team of five riders, ten horses with five grooms to Rome or Madrid today costs £2,500; each year we need nearly £15,000 solely for sending jumping teams overseas. To get this money our own International Shows have to thrive and attract the public. I know we were the first to realise the value of international success in this field, for our ambassadors throughout the world have frequently written to the Foreign Secretary explaining how much it has meant for Britain having a winning team at, say, Rome, Geneva, Madrid or Aachen.

But where was the money to come from? Through Bob Hanson and Sam Marsh I got to know Mr and Mrs Robert Dean—and they have helped me endlessly these past years. Bob Dean, a great expert, taught me the meaning of so many terms I didn't understand. I don't know whether I should refer to him as a Promoter or a P.R.O., but he and his wife have certainly been my friends. To begin with we had raffles, and flag days at Badminton, until some of Master's sheep unfortunately became supporters by getting flag pins stuck in their feet. However, we got through the first two or three years, and then Bob persuaded Mr Rank to give us the première of a film at the Plaza Cinema: Somerset Maugham's *Encore* starring Glynis Johns. It was a huge success with all the 'horse world' buying tickets from £15 down (it would be more now); everyone expected to wear pink evening coats, and we did. To my horror, Bob made me make an opening appeal, and this was filmed sitting on the stage at his studio. Afterwards we went to Ciro's, where Bob had arranged a fabulous supper. There were two bands and a cabaret and, 'square dancing' being very popular at that time, Master with Glynis Johns and others went to the cellars to learn their square dance as part of the cabaret.

We needed £8,000 to fly our team to Helsinki, and as a result of this première we had it. Bob said to me: 'Now win the Gold Medals and it will be worth £40,000 to you!'

In these vital years, our first Nations Cup to be taken by a civilian team was won at Geneva. The team included Wilf White with his Nizefela, and although that horse never really hit the headlines in individual championships the partnership remained our sheet anchor for many years—in fact I called Wilf the 'full back' of any of our Nations Cup wins. Pat Smythe had her twenty-first birthday party at the same Show. In years to come she was our finest ambassadress perhaps: she rode superbly, won every competition open to lady riders, and became the first woman to win an Olympic Equestrian Show-Jumping medal, at Stockholm in 1956. To me, Pat was far more than a great horsewoman: she enjoyed mixing with everyone, loved looking at beautiful pictures, visiting art galleries and, most impressive of all, I think, took the trouble to learn foreign languages. She speaks French, German and Spanish fluently, and a certain amount of Italian. One year she came to my home Show, Bideford, and afterwards we all went to bathe and lie in the sun at Westward Ho! Pat was reading a book and I asked her what it was. 'A Spanish Grammar,' she said. 'I'm learning Spanish.'

Mary Marshall with Nobbler came to the fore at about this time, so little wonder that I proposed Lady Riders should be admitted to Olympic Show-Jumping. But that didn't happen until 1956. Mr 'Ruby' Holland-Martin was rising with his Aherlow, until a tragic accident in the hunting field crippled him. Before that appalling mishap, when Harry Llewellyn won the 1949 Grand Prix at *Le Jumping* in Paris we all went afterwards to a celebration at some night club. It was Victoria's and my wedding anniversary, and after an excellent and expensive supper, when the bill arrived I asked what would be our share. Mrs Llewellyn, Teenie, looked at the bill, blinked (I almost heard it), and said, 'Golly, there are so many commas I don't think you should bother. After all, "Ruby" is a director of the Bank of England and Harry's a director of many ventures—they will be able to count the commas and pay the bill!'

The plan progressed in 1950, and out of four Nations Cups we won three. Peter Robeson had joined the team of future possibles with Craven A (that might now be forbidden, or the tobacco firm would have to pay a substantial sum): a superb horseman with a style second to none. That autumn we sent a team to America and Canada and they won no fewer than twelve individual competitions. By 1951 we were attacking on all fronts with more and more horses, though Foxhunter inevitably skimmed the cream with thirty-seven International wins in nine countries over two years, including the King's

Cup for the second time in 1950. So it is hardly surprising that the membership of the B.S.J.A. should have risen from 500 in 1944 to 10,000 by 1951.

Most gratifying from my own point of view, at the end of these packed three years, the turning point in my life, as I've said: both the International Horse Show at the White City and the Horse of the Year Show were drawing large crowds, and, above all, paid their way.

23

1952—Gold

When Her Majesty made me a C.B.E. in the New Year's Honours List of 1952, the honour was undoubtedly shared by all concerned with what 'the horse' had done to raise the prestige of Great Britain in recent years. We had at last realised the importance of victory in order to retain our reputation as horsemen. It wasn't enough to rest on our laurels by being good in the hunting field. During our tour of the North American circuit it had been realised how much the Americans liked winners—consequently the British Team was very popular. Seconds, thirds and hard-luck stories mean nothing, I fear. And I know many people don't like to face that.

At Porlock, the Three-Day Team got into their stride rather later than the jumpers, trained by Tony Collings and Wätjen of Germany. We'd learned or were learning the necessity of holding our own in the Dressage. Apart from the South American teams we'd met nearly every nation in the last two years, and believed our chief opponents at Helsinki would be Italy and Spain. At our last 'trial' event, Lucerne, we didn't jump either Foxhunter or Nizefela because they'd already selected themselves; the only problem was choosing the third rider: should it be Lt-Colonel Duggie Stewart of the Scots Greys, Alan Oliver or Peter Robeson? I had, in this case, the distinctly unenviable task of being Chairman of the Selection Committee. Finally, Duggie Stewart with E. Holland-Martin's Aherlow was chosen, Peter Robeson with his Craven A as reserve rider. So the die was cast. It is always wretched having to disappoint people by dropping them, as I knew only too well from my own feelings at being dropped from the English Polo Team in 1936.

The horses would have taken five days to send by sea, so we decided to fly them, each in a crate fitted with a belly band to stop them trying to lie down if the plane dropped suddenly. No problems except at take-off, when we learnt it was better to cover the windows. The Three-Day Event Team travelled first: Reg Hindley with his own Speculation, Bertie Hill to ride Lt-Colonel Miller's Stella, and Major Rook with Mrs Baker's Starlight. I flew out as *Chef d'Equipe* accompanied by Jack Webber.

When Jack and I arrived, we gave a taxi driver an address—supposedly of our lodgings. He seemed surprised. We were equally surprised on arriving at what might be termed the slums of Helsinki: the flat was at the top of a six-storied building, and when after repeated forlorn ringings a lady appeared, although without English she intimated beyond doubt that we were neither expected nor wanted. Well, here we were in Finland with nowhere to go, but we clung on to our friendly taxi driver and decided the best thing would be to seek out Reg Brown, Secretary of the B.H.S., and our Three-Day Team in the Olympic Village. Which we did, and by doubling up a room, Jack and I shared a small 'council' house with the cycling team due to return on the morrow. The Village was a new building site, the little houses hitherto unoccupied. Anyway, Jack and I were comfortable. We put down newspaper to soak up the damp sweating through the concrete.

As at all Olympic Games, the first of the three Equestrian events was the Dressage, in which we took no part; secondly the Three-Day, and lastly the Show-Jumping. The terrain for the Three-Day Cross-Country was flat and good sandy going, mainly arable, most of the trees silver birch. Jack Webber walked me round the course so that I could get the feel of it; the fences were well built and very solid, all birch. No team completed the course without falls over these fences except the German and our own. In the Three-Day Dressage we were ninth, just over half-way up. The second day, always the crucial part, with its endurance test, started at 7.00 a.m. It was to be quite a drama.

Our first two riders, Reg Hindley and Bertie Hill, completed the twenty-one-mile course well, and by that time ten teams had been eliminated: when Lawrence Rook riding Starlight set out, we knew that if only they could complete we must be in the money for a medal. Almost to the last, reports indicated they were doing well, when suddenly John Oram dashed up to say poor Lawrence had had a crashing fall on the flat. Then Lawrence himself appeared, covered in dirt and blood, started to dismount, but was pushed back and made to dismount in the unsaddling enclosure; he was obviously badly concussed and had in fact been knocked out. It transpired that, approaching the last fence, he'd swung off track to avoid a tree branch and Starlight caught his foot in a drain, stumbled out and fell into another. Although only barely returned to consciousness, Lawrence had been put up by some Finnish soldiers, and all might have been well, for he wasn't in the penalty zone. He jumped the last fence, and veered off into a cornfield— Harry Llewellyn saw it, went off to rescue him, and brought him back—he went the wrong side of the flag, and was disqualified.

Sweden first, Germany and the U.S.A. second and third. But for Lawrence's evil stars, we would have been Silver Medallists. So our feelings can be imagined when the most glorious sun lit the final day, the Grand Prix for

Show-Jumping—the last competition and Britain's last chance of a Gold Medal. Jack and I were in the stadium at 6.00 a.m. We met Jack Talbot-Ponsonby and the team. That phrase 'to do battle' really meant something, and battle it was to be: Harry and I and others had planned and waited four years for this day.

Twenty nations were entered, and each of the three horses of a team had to jump twice: once in the morning and again in the afternoon. Thirteen obstacles, comprising in all sixteen fences. I always liked to walk a course, feeling the size of the obstacles with the help of my stick, and Jack carefully took me round, giving a vivid description of each. It started with two what I call 'invitation fences' of brush and rails—an appetiser for what was to come. I can still remember that course in detail to this day. After the first two fences, a rider swung left across a diagonal of three fences that followed fairly quickly: the first parallel bars of 4 ft 9 in. with a 5-ft spread, then a post and rails of 4 ft 9 in., and, after, two sets of bright yellow planks standing 4 ft 8 in. with a wide spread of some 6 ft. This fence gave trouble: very *starey* and standing out in an already bright arena. The rider then turned right down the end of the arena, coming up on the outside to meet a difficult treble of a post and rails, followed by an open water of 9 ft, then a log wall 5 ft high, and only thirty-four feet from the water. The last fence down this side what we term a triple of brush, built like a triple bar with brush under each bar: nearly 5 ft high with a 7-ft spread. It caused endless trouble, and a Japanese fell into it—which held everything up for twenty minutes while major repairs were carried out. Having jumped this, you swung across the end of the arena and back on the right diagonal to meet what became a 'bogey': a double of rustic gates 4 ft 7 in. high with a 7-ft spread, followed after twenty-four feet by parallel bars, 4 ft 6 in., with a brush in the middle; this double followed immediately by a cream wall, 5 ft 3 in., then a bank of flowers with a rail standing 4 ft 10 in. The rider then swung left down the far side to be confronted by the water, a full 16 ft wide, followed only ninety feet away by a straight high gate of 5 ft 3 in. Aherlow was the only horse to jump these two fences without fault in the two rounds. The rider then gratefully turned left to the last fence, appropriately number 13, a bank of superb flowers with a rail at 4 ft 10 in. and a spread of over 7 ft.

By the time Jack and I had walked it I could visualise the whole thing easily. I anticipated the yellow planks would give trouble, also both combinations: a formidable course, but superbly built, and the width of the fences seemed to make them look easier.

As we climbed to our seats about 8.00 a.m. I just wondered, 'Could we do it?' We didn't know the form of the South American teams; I believed Italy would be our chief danger; possibly the Americans, who'd trained in Germany; Germany itself an unknown quantity.

Our first to jump was Aherlow ridden by Colonel Duggie Stewart. He went confidently and completed with twelve faults, having hit the third fence, the first on the diagonal and both parts of the double. Three fences down. This was all right, as we reckoned him possibly the number three. Nizefela ridden by Wilf jumped brilliantly, just within his time and round with four faults. He hit the gate after the water: distinctly odd, because although he only touched it we in England believed we could jump gates. In the early days, when wanting badly to win a competition at the International Horse Show, I fear that at the 'jump off' I was always apt to say, 'The gate up two' (six inches). Our friends from overseas soon learnt to jump gates.

The two first horses of each team having jumped, Italy led with twelve faults, we and Portugal were equal second with sixteen. Jack and I felt we were set fair, with Foxhunter to come. Then the real drama of this tense morning: Piero d'Inzeo of Italy riding Uruguay didn't appear. He was called; a wait of one minute; the bell sounded; and our main opponents were out of the hunt. I was desperately sorry for Piero: a fine horseman—stupid on this occasion, for after being called to the 'inner pocket' to wait his turn he'd left to have one more practice jump outside, and wasn't allowed back. Jack gave me a whispered commentary as each horse came into the arena: 'Over 1, over 2, now turning to 3. He's too close—it's down!' ('Thank Heavens,' under my breath, I'm ashamed to say.)

And now Foxhunter was in the ring, Jack quietly saying he looked very 'perky', not settled. He jumped the first four fences clean, but going too slowly for him, not jumping with his usual confidence—and down came those yellow planks. Four faults gone. He jumped the double, going much too slow, cleared the wall almost from a halt—how, I'll never know—stopped at the bank of flowers, and how Harry stayed *on* I shall never know: he got his spur hooked into Foxhunter's girth, but managed to get back into the saddle. The horse then hit the bank of flowers, an easy fence, and already had eleven faults. Jumped the water with ease, hit the gate, cleared the last fence: with 'time' faults added, a total of $16\frac{3}{4}$. Hell, I thought, a lot of good my prayers and sitting on my handkerchief for luck had done!

By the end of the morning session the score stood: U.S.A. 23, Portugal 24, Argentine 28, Brazil $28\frac{1}{2}$, Germany 32, Great Britain $32\frac{3}{4}$, Spain 35, France, Sweden and Mexico 36. Fritz Thiedermann of Germany on Meteor had jumped the only clear round. Meteor had competed in the Grand Prix Dressage, and it surely underlined the truth that, to win, you must also school your horses on the flat. We went to luncheon; Jack quite calm, but though I didn't show it I was very despondent and felt we'd thrown the thing away. It was 'help yourselves' in the main restaurant, and we certainly did that in an effort to console ourselves. Then Jack produced a mass of telegrams for me, but unfortunately most of them mentioned 'Dear' Fox-

131

hunter. I fear at that time we quietly felt he deserved a good thump not a pat. We had two or three hours before the renewal of the contest, and while the riders rightly relaxed and slept, and Jack Talbot-Ponsonby went to the stables to ensure that Foxhunter got some exercise and not be so 'full of himself' as in the morning, I settled at the typewriter to compose a rather despondent article for my friend Walter Case of *Horse and Hound*. As we know in the Army, work is a vital factor in times of crisis!

By three-fifteen the stadium was bursting with 80,000 people. Almost immediately the Argentines were out of the hunt—their first horse went lame. Wrongly, I suppose, I sighed with relief. Duggie Stewart did a superb round with Aherlow: only four faults, shooting us up to second place behind the U.S.A. Wilf White on dear Nizefela jumped splendidly, unlucky to have four faults knocked down to him at the water. There was much doubt about this—only one of the two judges put up his flag, and personally I'm convinced he didn't go in but landed in the overflow caused by previous horses—it is sometimes difficult to distinguish the splash from the water proper. How I longed for the 1948 games and the Wembley Water Shortage! When Russell of the U.S.A. on Democrat finished with sixteen faults I just said THANK YOU. I'm not prepared to disclose to whom I said it. We were now in the lead, with one horse from each nation to jump, and the tension was just about too much. I prayed and sat on more handkerchiefs for luck. Teenie (Mrs Harry Llewellyn) and Harry's mother couldn't bear it, so went to the loo. When Harry entered with Foxhunter, he could afford one mistake only, no more. After the disastrous morning of Foxhunter leaving with $16\frac{3}{4}$ faults and Harry with a bleeding nose, it needed a lot of nerve to will a clear round, but, as Jack quietly told me, they were different beings: Foxhunter had done an hour's work, Harry had had an hour's sleep. 'One clear. He's jumping superbly. Two clear. Three clear—no worry there!' I prayed, but I knew we were home and dry, and as he jumped the last fence I cheered. Many hadn't computed as quickly as I, but we'd won. The last Chilean rider also jumped a clear round, edging out the U.S.A. team from second place.

At home the family had been very miserable when they knew the lunch-time score. Assembled at tea-time, they heard Raymond Glendenning announce that Britain's only Gold Medal had been won in the last event of the Helsinki Games. Victoria burst into tears, and Sarah said, 'Mummy, what's the matter? I thought you wanted Daddy's team to win? We have won. Why cry?'

A telegram received by the Duke of Beaufort hangs proudly in my study. It reads as follows:

> Handed in at Windsor Castle 3.5 on August 4th 1952. To the Duke of Beaufort, Helsinki.

My mother, Margaret and I send heartiest congratulations to Mike Ansell and the Jumping Team on their magnificent win and a special pat to Foxhunter.

Elizabeth R.

The riders and horses returned home to a great welcome, though unfortunately, as always, too much was made of their relative share in the victory. Had Nizefela or Foxhunter been crucial? Wilf or Harry? Harry on Foxhunter had scored the winning goal, but what did it matter? In actual fact, Duggie Stewart's second round with Aherlow was crucial. But if we're bored we'll be arguing about that sort of thing to eternity, in paradise, limbo or hell.

The Royal International Horse Show started on August 18, and the crowd stood and cheered as each of the three Gold Medallists received a pair of gold spurs. Nothing succeeds like success, we know: 80,000 people attended the show, giving us a profit of £3,700.

I was glad to get home and away from everything, particularly the telephone. For some years I used to take the family to a small hotel at Two Bridges in the middle of Dartmoor, and we rarely lacked excitement on the journey by car: we were usually stopped at road blocks while warders made sure there were no escaped convicts hidden away in the boot. Victoria and I walked a great deal in this wild and rugged country which is so different from Exmoor. The children fished, Sarah often with a bare hook: she couldn't be bothered with worms. Much to my disapproval, Nicholas, I found, had set a night line for trout on this occasion. He got two large ones, excellent to eat, but he didn't set night lines again on Dartmoor.

As that summer ended I was conscious that a very important period in my life also drew to its close. Now I had accustomed myself to a life of not seeing, and our horsemen raced along the road to success.

24

Marketing Our Wares

The winning of the Helsinki Gold Medal did much for me personally: it gave me great confidence in my dealings with the British Show-Jumping Association, and for that matter with the British Horse Society and the two Shows. In the early days of the International Horse Show, Olympia, as it was known then, money mattered little. There were many fairy godfathers under the Earl of Lonsdale's umbrella, and for the privilege of calling themselves vice-presidents they were only too happy to make good any loss—thus ensuring that Olympia continued as a fabulous social event in all its glory. But even in the 1930s, change was worming to the surface: an answer hadn't been found, and one year the Show had to be cancelled altogether on account of the previous year's heavy loss. As I've said before, I felt I knew how the problem should be solved, and at the right time I met people like Bob Dean, Ruby Holland-Martin, Bob Hanson and Cecil Murray—people with business brains who could guide me. Bob Dean in particular would always be needling: 'Was our image right? Surely I must know the difference between advertising and Public Relations . . .? Surely it was time to carry out a survey as to why and from where our supporters came . . . ?' It took me a little time to understand this kind of language (some might say, lingo) but I learnt. And I knew that a winning team of International riders was something worth 'marketing'. So crowds grew at the White City and Harringay; so did the profits. Better production; more wins abroad—until one morning Bob might say, 'Surely you realise you must get greater spectator participation?' After reeling a bit from those ugly polysyllables, I would think about it. Dorian Williams, that superb commentator (although at times I called him a mere announcer), was always full of advice, later joined by Raymond Brooks-Ward, who helped me make a success of the Mounted Games—and these last greatly increased 'spectator enthusiasm'.

By organising our affairs commercially we've been able to raise the prize money for the jumping events at the Royal International Horse Show from £1,700 in 1953 to nearly £15,000 in 1972. This increase has made it possible for riders from all walks of life to compete and up to a point pay their way. That is the real 'revolution'. The bait has inevitably encouraged the breeders, as the right type of horse became more valuable. The great essential will always be to win International competitions.

In many parts of the world it doesn't seem to matter whether the Show makes a profit or not: some are subsidised by hotels as a tourist attraction, others by casinos and still others by their Government, but I remain convinced it's better to stand on your own feet and escape being controlled by some outside body.

Now B.B.C. Television became interested in our two Shows. For a couple of years negotiations were in the hands of Mr Frank Gentle, and I fear I disagreed with him, for he was convinced that if we showed our best championships, or the finish of a competition, the 'gate' would drop. I fought, believing we must show nothing but the best—and what is more exasperating than being cut off just before a dramatic finish? Eventually the negotiating was left to the two Bobs (Hanson and Dean) and me. Our fee soon went up to £4,000, until one day Peter Dimmock of the B.B.C. asked us to lunch at the Normandie Hotel and Bob Hanson told me in the taxi-cab that Peter was about to offer us £8,000. 'We're having nothing of that,' he said breezily. Sure enough, after the usual superb luncheon, Peter purred, 'Now to business. Hold on to your seats, you'll both be so surprised.' 'Go ahead,' murmured Bob. When Peter duly made his £8,000 offer, Bob enquired blankly, 'But why hold on to our seats? We're having nothing of that.' We all settled happily for £10,000. It is nice to remember that a very few years before we were paid £340 for both Shows. Today we can add a couple of noughts.

We had the great advantage over other sports of being able to run live during peak viewing hours, and even then we drew millions to their screens. At the present time, viewing figures for the two Wembley Shows vary between nine and thirteen and a half million on each of the six nights.

Show-jumping was a 'cinch' for television: comparatively easy to cover, because the producer knew where the rider was going. Cricket, football or any ball game is quite a different matter. I've been particularly lucky in recent years to have Alan Mouncer as producer: he always seems to know what I'm hoping for. Naturally, in the wake of being televised came the offers from various great organisations to sponsor us: that needed very careful handling, and again Bob Dean guided me.

The renaming of championships after certain sponsors proved a very tricky point. Understandably, many people objected that our horse sports should be commercialised, but I do believe they were short-sighted or that they refused to perceive the true objective: it was essential for the future of this sport that, potentially, everyone could participate, whatever their funds.

I'm sure I don't need to emphasise how much time and effort all this took, so it was hardly surprising that Victoria should be constantly suggesting (and that is a mild way of putting it) that I would be better employed making these large profits for the family. Although the garden grew and I now had three men working for me, it certainly didn't show a profit; but in those days the Tax Inspector was kind and allowed the loss to go against my tax. In addition to the selling of Gerberas and seed, we'd started to market gladiolus. We used to show at Exeter and Taunton, and our gladiolus used to be shown as a bed. I had any amount of small pipes, about an inch in diameter; these had corks at one end, were placed in the ground and filled with water; a gladiolus was popped into each pipe and they looked entirely natural. We then started a mail-order business, and we'd send our customers an attractive Christmas card stating that a gift of gladiolus would arrive in the spring. It provided a large turnover, but week-ends in February I didn't much enjoy packing and sending out the gifts of corms.

Victoria and I went to many of the places where our riders were competing. Lucerne, Rome, Madrid, Aachen, Dublin, New York, Toronto—each has its own character if only one can avoid the airports. I think everyone agrees that airports are too similar: no longer that leisurely drift through Customs, the smell of some strange tobacco or exotic cooking. Rome is my favourite. That wonderful Piazza da Sienna, superb going on sand, the giant pine trees—each a sorceress applauding and bewailing success or defeat. Perhaps it is nostalgia because I so enjoyed my Show in 1939, before the whole world blew apart. Ranieri Campello and his charming wife Maria Sole were very great friends, and we often stayed with them at Castel Lombardo, but in the ring Maria Sole and I could never sit together—such was our fervent partisanship for our respective sides. Harry Llewellyn always loved Rome too, and when not performing used to give me a running commentary. As one of our opponents came in I would hear, 'Over 1, over 2' and so on until, if the rider was doing too well, we'd decide he must be made to fault at whichever number fence. Harry would say, 'Wait, let me do it.' I'd sit on my handkerchief, as usual, praying. Harry pointed both fingers at the unfortunate opponent and, 'DOWN,' we'd say—and sure enough, down it would come. Even Harvey Smith once said to Harry, 'I didn't think the Colonel minded so much about our winning.' Once when I wasn't there, Harry on Foxhunter was last in our team. To win he had to clear the water and a very high wall: alas, one foot went in the water and the Nations Cup was lost. The Italian supporters rose and cheered, Harry ironically raised his hat in acknowledgement—and cleared the last fence. Unfortunately some of our friends in the Press made much of this gesture, and Harry cabled me his apologies. I just wired back, 'Nothing to worry about so long as your hair was cut.' His always was.

In 1953 at Rome we were staying with our ambassador, Sir Victor Mallet and his wife (old friends of Victoria's—and it was they who'd sought me out ten years before on my repatriation at Göteborg). Our team wasn't doing well, and Sir Victor, sceptical, usually hurried off to the Open Tennis Championships. But on the day of the Grand Prix he was there, and our luck was in. Bill Hanson, a brilliant young rider, who'd recently risen, was one of only two to jump a clear round (on The Monarch), the other an Italian. So, with our ambassador there, drama. With perfect determination Bill jumped a second clean and took the Rome Grand Prix: the only time we've ever won it. It was devastating when this splendid rider died a year later. A real loss to this country.

Sometimes we went to the Madrid Show—again very different: an arena decorated with glorious roses, and the 'pace' very leisurely. After every ten horses there had to be an interval while spectators made their choice of the next ten and put their money on the Tote. Victoria was marvellous at all these places because, as I've said, she could speak the languages or at any rate tried, unlike me. Consequently it was I who proposed the resolution that English be included as an official language of the F.E.I.! Once when we arrived at the Madrid Show ground Victoria noticed that the Union Jack on the British Ambassador's box was hanging upside down. With the help of an official and a pair of pincers she removed the tacks and put it the right way up. Just as well perhaps, for we won the Nations Cup. They then took me to meet General Franco. I was impressed: a quiet yet strong personality. The Show drifted on its leisurely way, everybody was charming, but oh, those late nights . . .

From there to Lisbon, and the horses and grooms had a slow and difficult journey. Victoria and I had to come home early and the riders wondered if I could do anything to make their return trip easier. So I wrote to General Franco explaining how much we had enjoyed his Show in Madrid, and winning his Nations Cup, but that we had not enjoyed his railways so much, and could he please do something to accelerate our return. The horses certainly passed quickly over the frontier, hardly stopping to shunt from one express to another. I'm afraid the next complaint came from the owners: their horses had travelled too fast, and had been rocketed about.

As a member of the Bureau of the *Fédération Equestre Internationale*, I attended all meetings, and fortunately at that time there were two other members of my own age, Ranieri Campello, an old comrade, and Arne Franke of Sweden. They both had charming wives, and the six of us used to dine together each evening and 'plot' our next day's business. Général Baron de Trannoy was our President, and he couldn't have been nicer, though I fear he lived in the clouds. In 1954 I proposed, again, that non-commissioned officers should be permitted to compete in the Olympic Games. Fortunately I had Group-Captain Peter Townsend with me to steer me around and act as interpreter. He had a great sense of humour and ably translated the Général's speech against my proposition. He ended by saying,

'If non-commissioned officers were allowed to compete, how could the social standard be maintained? What would happen at the receptions?' Peter Townsend told me to say nothing, but to look down as the Général was showing the whites of his eyes. It was put to the vote as 'Ansell versus the Bureau'. Luckily, Ranieri and Arne backed me, and Ansell won. Non-commissioned officers were allowed to compete in the Olympic Equestrian Events of 1956.

25

Some Royal Occasions

Nobody one of my children ever seemed to be bored or want to sit about, do nothing, watch television. Nicholas loved wild-fowling, particularly at home in the Taw and Torridge Estuary: he used to go off very early in the cold January mornings, and on one such occasion, with Antony, they shot three widgeon, all of which dropped into the estuary. Although the tide was going out, Nicholas stripped off everything, except my wrist-watch, and swam after them; he retrieved two but finding the swimming difficult wisely turned back—then put his clothes on and went after snipe with his brother.

By 1955 Nicholas had become head of Wellington and he then passed into both Oxford and Cambridge—choosing the latter, to be near good wild-fowling in Norfolk, and also because it's close to Newmarket. First, of course, he had to do his National Service: in his case with the Inniskillings. Antony didn't want to go to university and did his stint with the 12th Lancers, for my regiment would not accept brothers. I think, wisely: in war difficult problems can arise from that situation.

Three-Day Eventing grew rapidly, and a very broad base of riders and horses was being built up as with Show-Jumping. Tragically, Tony Collings was killed in the first Comet disaster. That would be 1954, and we could ill afford to lose such a tremendous enthusiast. Badminton went from strength to strength, and there Victoria and I had the privilege of getting to know Her Majesty and Prince Philip, with other members of the Royal Family. In that same year, 1954, the Queen suggested holding the Three-Day Event at Windsor the following year in order to give Master's land a rest. Naturally, the Royal Park provided an ideal setting, though it posed some problems for the course designer: fences had to be rather more artificial; 'island' fences standing out on their own. There was a 'house party' at Windsor Castle, and Queen Elizabeth the Queen Mother asked us to stay at Royal Lodge, to make things easier for me. What fun we had each evening, with Princess Margaret playing the piano and entertaining us in her inimitable fashion. From one of her songs, I learnt always to refer to the 'telephone', and since then I've taken pleasure in saying to my friends, 'You mean telephone, not phone. And please do not give me a ring.' I was being properly educated at last. One day at luncheon I sat next to the Queen: we had cold salmon, and I seemed to have a mass of knives. I was feeling about for the right one, I thought a fish knife, when the Queen said, laughing, 'Mike, they are all the same. No fish knives.' It must have been at this time that Princess Margaret quoted to me Sir John Betjeman's 'Phone for the fish knives, Norman'.

The Windsor Three-Day Event succeeded despite terrible weather that May. We even had to endure snow. Frank Weldon won it, riding Kilbarry, and Bertie Hill also did well on a new horse, Countryman. This horse was later most generously bought by the Queen, the Queen Mother, Master, and Colonel Vivian Williams *from* Bertie *for* Bertie to ride: he could not afford to keep so great a horse. On the last day, as we sat in the stand, young Prince Charles offered me a chocolate. Having removed the paper and put it into my hand, he enquired whether or not he should put it in my mouth. I think he seemed a little perplexed that someone who could not see was able to find his mouth.

The 'production' of the two big London shows became more complicated, requiring endless detailed planning which I thoroughly enjoyed. David Satow, John Blackmore and I spent hours working out the time table, then at home I would draft the myriad instructions. To me it was rather like planning an attack: in my case perhaps, as in 1940, a retirement. Even so, things would go wrong and that only added to the excitement. Since 1954 I've had Lawrence Rook to help me and steer me around, and he is a fund of efficiency and humour. In general the point is always to be ready to make a quick decision to get out of trouble. My friends have invariably accepted these decisions, knowing I have no axe to grind, own no horses, and merely do what I believe to be correct.

There are mistakes certainly. I'll never forget in 1954 when Fritz Thiedermann riding Meteor had won the King's Cup at the White City, in the presence of the Queen. Although the Director of Music had specific written instructions always to play the winner's National Anthem from the bandstand, to my horror I heard Lawrence whispering, 'The something band has formed up in the middle of the arena.' We realised the Director of Music had forgotten he would have to play the German National Anthem, without music, in the dark. If it weren't played, there would be a question from the German Embassy. 'Hell,' I thought. But I was saved, for the ever watchful Captain Wally Eyres R.N., General Manager of the White City, was striding towards the Director. Wally had boxed for the Navy and played rugger for England: he did not suffer mistakes.

'Play the German Anthem, you fool,' said Wally, his fist stuck in the Director's ribs.

'I can't,' said the Director, 'we've no music . . .'

'Play something, you something fool,' came Wally's determined whisper. Luckily, the unfortunate Director knew the anthem, so he whistled it, the band took it up, and while he conducted something rather weird came out. That night the Queen came back to Kensington Palace with Master and the Duchess of Beaufort. The Queen quietly said to me, with a laugh, 'Mike, your band sounded a bit odd tonight.'

Weather, beyond everything, can provide the most awful hazards, but I've never cancelled a performance. The worst, I think, came in 1964, at the White City. Between an afternoon and evening performance, at about six, the 'heavens opened' and within half an hour the whole ring was a lake—the fences stood by their own reflections when the lights came on. Lawrence and I took one look and I said, 'Come along to my room.' We got on our gum boots, had a large whisky and soda, and pondered. As so often happens, the storm over, it was a lovely evening. Dare we go on? Everything else in London, the Alexandra Palace Race Meeting, Harringay Greyhound Racing, etc., had been cancelled. I decided to take a gamble and Lawrence agreed. 'Cancel the first jumping competition, the evening performance will start at eight. All stewards to be found and told. The whole arena to be sanded with the help of wheelbarrows—obviously no tractors to be brought on. All the "show" classes to be judged on the running track.'

Master came in to ask what I was going to do, as the Princess Royal had telephoned to ask if it had been cancelled. When I told him, I think Master thought I was mad. The band of the Inniskillings had started as instructed at six forty-five for the seven o'clock opening. I called over to Mr Howe, smart in his green overalls, shouting that he was to play lively music till eight o'clock. Poor Mr Howe couldn't hear, and smartly handing his baton to the Sergeant-Major, he hurried over. Unfortunately he'd forgotten that the permanent steeplechase water-jump lay between us, now merged with the lake, and into it he almost disappeared. He came out smiling, saluted smartly, and learnt he was to 'play like hell' until eight o'clock for those arrived and waiting. 'Very good, Colonel. May I change my overalls?'—and with a laugh he left. My luck was in. That night we had one of the best jumping competitions for many a day.

I suppose it was my Army life that taught me rather to enjoy a problem and having to get out of trouble. Another performance done, we'd usually be able to say, 'Well that's all right, hurrah.' And Lawrence would steer me deftly through the crowd, whispering perhaps, 'Keep walking, so-and-so is coming up. He looks a bit upset.' One advantage of being blind is that with Lawrence's help I can avoid difficult encounters without seeming rude. Back in my room, Victoria or I might say, 'One more night, then home and to our hide-out on Dartmoor!'

141

26

Toronto and On

Through my old friend Bob Hanson I met Mr Hal Crang of Toronto. He was a great character, and incidentally Chairman of the Royal Winter Fair of Toronto, possibly the largest indoor Agricultural Show in the world. One day in 1955 I received a letter suggesting I come out to advise and help him that November. He asked what fee would be expected, and this rather floored me. I'd never had a fee for advising on a Show, so I wrote explaining that I did not want one. Later he explained that he, a stock-broker, obtained the best advice possible when launching a project, and expected to pay for it. Victoria and I went out to try and help Hal, but that wasn't easy: those who'd been organising the great show were not anxious for suggestions from some Englishman. This mammoth affair would hardly have attracted crowds in our country: the timing and production weren't exactly worried about. For a Show to run an hour or two late was nothing. From our point of view it was set twenty years back, with the emphasis still on '*élite*' spectators in the evening—pink tail-coats, white ties, full decorations and medals.

Hal was a 'go-getter'. Wandering around the Trade Stands, I might buy a small monkey mascot, whereupon Hal would buy a dozen—and then hurry off to order a dozen bottles of gin for a party in his office that morning. Suddenly he'd remember he'd forgotten to buy a motor-car—off he'd fly to the Bentley stand. Having chosen a model, he'd enquire if it was air-conditioned, and hearing it was not would say, 'Oh dear, it must be air-conditioned. If you can deliver one this afternoon by six o'clock, I will have it.' And at six o'clock the present for his wife Dorothy would be outside the house.

From time to time I'd remember that I was supposed to be advising, and tactfully make a suggestion or two. Nothing was 'leapt at' immediately, but many of my ideas have been taken up in recent years. Everything Hal himself did, though, he did flat-out. It was typical of him to have held for years the record of breaking a thousand clay pigeons within an hour, using three guns. I'm proud to say that I have many friends in Canada, but even when jumping there with the British Army Team we used to pull their legs—and at times I still do. In 1957 Victoria and I were over again. Master was judging the show on this occasion and the Duchess of Beaufort had gone with him. At a party one night, Mary Beaufort and Victoria were already there when Master and I arrived late. I immediately realised I was standing near the Duchess and pointedly asked her if by any chance she had met the Duchess of Beaufort. I then enquired what kind of an old woman Her Grace was and what she looked like. Mary, of course, plunged zealously into her description, explaining that the Duchess was an awful 'old frump'. My Canadian friends were exceedingly embarrassed and made frantic signs to Mary trying to indicate that I was blind and didn't realise to whom I was speaking. Well, of course, when blind, the one thing you learn to recognise is voices!

Three-Day Event riders were now making their mark. Although I had little to do with these and their success, as Honorary Director of the British Horse Society I was responsible for the money side, and I constantly tried to make the events pay their way—not always easy, as can be imagined. The Princess Royal, who always came to Badminton, had now started a Three-Day Event at Harewood, thus providing greater opportunity for our riders; and 'One-Day' events spread rapidly. Her Royal Highness was an inveterate anti-litter campaigner: I dread to think what she would have felt about some of our County Shows today. Each evening at Harewood an army of Girl Guides would move in. No scrap of paper or empty bottle survived long. Even at Badminton, evenings would see the Princess Royal accompanied by Victoria picking the rubbish out of the mud.

Post-war, my life has been marked in four-year periods governed by the Olympics, but 1956 had a personal importance for me too. Nicholas joined the Inniskillings, and having boxed at Wellington (although he disliked it as much as I did) was put in charge of the Regimental boxing team. He is the third Ansell to have served in the Inniskillings.

H.R.H. Prince Philip now became President of the British Horse Society, and I consider myself fortunate to have had the opportunity of getting to know him: on very many occasions, and in many different matters, I have been able to seek his help and guidance. One quickly realises that Prince Philip wants to know everything; and by his method of persistent, probing questions, he soon learns 'the lot'.

The next Olympic Games were due to be held in Melbourne, but owing to their quarantine restrictions the Australians could not accept the equestrian events, so for the first time it was decided to hold them, by themselves, in Stockholm: a most suitable venue, since Show-Jumping had first been included in the Stockholm Olympics of 1912. Fine also for us in the 'horse world': each four years the Olympics become larger and larger, and individual sports are gobbled up. We were now coming back into these equestrian events which in pre-war days, for some reason, we'd rather ignored; so, also for the first time, we were competing in all three events now that our Dressage had been brought up to standard.

W. S. Gilbert may rightly have written 'a policeman's lot is not a happy one': for the third time my 'lot' was that of Chairman of the Show-Jumping Selection Committee. And this time we defended our Gold Medal. It had always been my intention to send as many different riders as possible abroad; but money, as usual, caused its difficult problems, for many of our best riders preferred to jump in England, where prize money is high. Nevertheless we'd succeeded, and now in 1956 we had an embarrassing number of 'International' riders to choose from. The 'Three-Day' was easy, however: what we might call the 'Three-Day Pioneers' virtually choosing themselves: Frank Weldon with Kilbarry, Lawrence Rook riding Wild Venture and Bertie Hill with Countryman. The Show-Jumping Team was far from so easy, but to cut a tortuous story short we finally chose Wilf White with Nizefela, Pat Smythe with Flanagan and Peter Robeson with Scorchin. Inevitable criticism from the Press, of course; and how I hate selecting teams. My position with the B.H.S. and the B.S.J.A. meant that I was not only responsible for the teams but all those members who wished to support them—passages to and from, accommodation, etc. It was quite certain that more than one 'so-and-so' would land in the wrong hotel, and many were the rumbles and grumbles in Stockholm. In fact Victoria and I might have led the chorus, finding ourselves in an ultra-modern hotel: in our cabin, or cupboard, my bed let down out of the wall. But we were there to enjoy ourselves, and we did.

The Queen and Prince Philip were there with the Royal Yacht. There was an evening at the Royal Opera, a wonderful reception on *Britannia* and a delicious dinner with Prince Bertil—H.R.H. being a quite excellent chef who did not like guests arriving late. These Olympics were undoubtedly the happiest I have ever known, partly because of their scale away from the other events. The stadium, built for those Games of 1912, very attractive, with two red-brick towers, from one of which the Olympic Flame burned: hardly surprising that the rider who brought it had to dismount and take rather a time to climb the tower and light up at the top.

We ended the first phase of the Three-Day, the Dressage Test, well in the lead from Germany and Sweden. The first time we'd ever been in that position: a triumph due entirely to the training by Colonel and Mrs Williams. Our friends from overseas still thought we spent our time out hunting, so we were happy. Throughout the night it rained, and we expected the cross-country course to be flooded, but the organisation was superb and the Swedish Army Engineers worked wonders. As the day wore on we were clearly going to finish well. Victoria and I steadily walked the whole course praying for success. The Queen and Prince Philip followed from fence to fence, and I know their presence stirred every member of the team as it did me. When Frank Weldon found himself in a position where he could ride for the Individual Gold Medal or, by taking no risks, for the Team Gold Medal, he unselfishly chose the latter. By this time I was at the finish with scores coming in fast, and I'm afraid that in my usual way I cheered quietly when some opponent had a mishap—I so badly wanted our trio to win. We finished that day with a commanding lead, and our Show-Jumping on the morrow delivered the *coup de grâce*; our team with ease Gold Medallists, with Frank Weldon taking the Individual Bronze.

And so to Sunday, and the traditional last event of the Games, the Grand Prix. Even in Show-Jumping much runs to form, and in 1955 we had not won a single Nations Cup. Nevertheless we expected the battle to be between Germany, Italy and Britain, and it was. When we arrived at 7.00 a.m. in that perfect stadium the arena appeared packed full of fences—seventeen in all—because the area was smaller than at Helsinki or Wembley. The going was sticky from overnight rain, clear rounds at a premium therefore; but the major problem was two lines of five fences at difficult distances. This meant that horse and rider had to 'attack' from the start: tackle each fence individually and impetus would be lost. Victoria and I rather naturally sat with Maria Sole and Ranieri Campello, and equally naturally, of course, Maria Sole sat well away from me. Our lack of neutrality in the arena was too well established. Victoria and Ranieri (between us) were perfect diplomats and always 'sorry' when their opponents failed. Needless to say, we two were not. Behind us sat Monsieur Polyterniac, Vice-President of the *Fédération*, with his two sticks ready to express disapproval as much as to help him walk. Whenever a horse jumped the line in front of us, the spectators cheered; whenever a horse failed, some twenty to thirty poles came to the ground and our impatient Vice-President thumped the stand with both his sticks and loudly exclaimed: 'What can you expect from a country that makes matches!' The morning's first round of the twenty-five teams took nearly five hours—but much of that time was spent replacing the broken silver birch poles execrated by Monsieur Polyterniac.

Pat Smythe, the first lady rider to compete in an Olympic Grand Prix, had ridden Flanagan superbly to complete with only eight faults. Wilf White did the same on his reliable Nizefela. Germany led with 28 faults to our 32 and Italy's 39. The form book coming out fairly 'true'. It soon became apparent in the afternoon that Germany was going to win. Hans Winkler had torn a riding muscle during the morning, but with perfect courage he went on though in great pain. Just as great was the performance of Halla, who took Hans out after the first faultless round. Our Peter Robeson with Scorchin had a round of 22 faults, and Pat 13 with the gallant

Flanagan. Wilf, as always our sheet-anchor, rose to the occasion with only four faults. The battle was now for the silver between Italy and ourselves—Raimondo and his brother Piero d'Inzeo edging us out by three points: greatly to Maria Sole's delight of course! Now we could happily be friends again. Germany the Gold, 40 faults; Italy the Silver, 66 faults; Britain the Bronze, 69 faults.

I won't pretend that it wasn't disappointing not to win, particularly with the Queen and Prince Philip there to cheer us on, but one can hardly sniff at a Bronze Medal. The debate will ever continue whether it is better to maintain a few riders on a few great horses, or encourage as many as possible to gain International recognition. I will always defend the second as being the better plan, and we in this country have stuck to it. More and more young riders go abroad each year, making new friends, seeing the world, and consequently we learn to understand each other.

Immediately the Games were over many left for home, but Victoria and I stayed, for the Swedish Federation had organised an International Jumping Show—and with a few days interval we seized the opportunity to see something of the country. I was now a proud fisherman of one year's standing, and wanted to try the legendary Swedish rivers for their sea trout. After motoring over three hundred miles, we arrived at our log cabin, obligingly near a wide river. Fishing had been arranged, but the fish had not been warned to be present. For two days I sat in a boat with a rod, various large flies trolling behind, while my boatman explained that either the water was not 'right', or there was too much sun—anyway conditions were all wrong. I now know this is quite a common explanation of fishing woes; fortunately I mostly only remember the good days. Evenings were fully occupied trying to persuade our log fire to smoke—to discourage the hordes of mosquitoes. Victoria was badly bitten by these: there's no doubt that those blessed with fair skin and hair are cursed in that way. Happily, after a couple of days in bed she was much better, in time to enjoy the greatest Nations Cup Show-Jumping competition I have *ever* witnessed.

The Nations Cup draws teams of four not three, though only the top three scores count, and Dawn Palethorpe with Earlsrath Rambler joined Wilf, Peter and Pat. Sixty-eight competitors had to jump two rounds; and fortunately the summer days are long in Sweden, for the contest took nearly ten hours. But that was not the end. Britain had tied with our old rivals Italy, and we had to endure a long interval while they prepared the course for the jump-off. The excitement became unbearable. Rider after rider entered, yet we still were level, until, incredibly, Merano refused and ran out, unseating poor Raimondo. What a good thing Maria Sole wasn't there.

The magnificent cup bearing the Royal Coat of Arms of H.M. the King of Sweden stands in my office. That night we all dined together, and fortunately Betty Whitbread had stayed on and joined us: the only guest. This time, unlike the celebration at Helsinki, we had between us sufficient money to pay the bill without going to our Embassy!

27

━━◆◆◆◆━━

Fishing Blind

This seems a good point to tell of how I came to take up my 'ultimate' sport. Before the war, although I did a little shooting, what with polo, hunting and point-to-pointing, not to speak of my work, I'd never had time to give serious thought to fishing. Then after the war I seemed to have a full life, and I didn't think fishing particularly suitable for one who couldn't see. Unexpectedly, Ian Fraser told me about his own enthusiasm for fishing, particularly with a fly, and so in 1956 I decided to 'have a go'.

I wanted to catch fish, and made no bones about it! Although many of the more '*élite*' fishermen look down on spinning, I determined not only to be a fly fisherman but also to spin.

If you cannot see, fishing with a fly is the easier because once you have the distance and the angle right, you're safe from landing on the far bank or getting hitched up in the bottom. When spinning in a narrow river, there's always the anxiety of getting far enough over and yet not too far. Practice and more practice is the only answer. And I found my best method was to aim at a tin tray on the lawn; with a small weight on the line, I could hear when it found its mark. Gradually I became more efficient until I could land on the tray five times out of seven. Lord Fraser, as I've said, was a fly fisherman; an annual bet of a sovereign each year on who caught the most salmon finally persuaded him to take notice of spinning. By that time his sovereign had become a regular part of my income, and certainly was not declared for tax.

St Dunstan's always had an expert whose task was to provide some means of achieving almost anything when blind—without fingers or even without arms. At that time it was Mr Nye, and one morning he came round to my office to check over a tape-recorder. Quietly he quizzed me as to how I practised spinning, and when I told him he said he knew all about that: Lord Fraser had gone one better, for Mr Nye had fixed up a drum with an amplifier so that Ian could hear when he landed on target. 'However,' added Mr Nye, 'on no account must you tell his Lordship, but yesterday evening I went round to St John's Lodge to see how things were getting on, and found one of the grandchildren on the roof unravelling his Lordship's line from around the chimney.'

Obviously a blind fisherman must have a gillie with him. It is he who encourages and is so thrilled when you land a fish, he who can do everything possible to get you one, and equally, if you know it all and say so, he's quite happy to let you get on with it and catch nothing. I well remember a particularly cold day on the Tweed at Cornhill when I was fortunate enough to get five. I couldn't understand why the fisherman of the previous day had got nothing, but when I asked the reply was brief: 'Oh, Mr Blank knew it all. I let him get on with it, remembering we would be together today.'

I believe that a blind person is in some ways better off than the sighted for salmon fishing, provided he can cast accurately. When spinning, as I obviously don't see the line stop if a fish takes hold, I wait till I feel it with my finger on the line and so don't tighten too soon. In the same way, with a fly I cannot see that tantalising swirl as the fish rises. I have to wait, and that wait till the fish has taken is crucial. Having been trained all my life in the army, I get directions by the clock. I know I must cast at 'one o'clock' i.e. slightly downstream, or if my friend the gillie says 'twelve o'clock' I know I'm too high, and if the order 'that's three o'clock' comes, I can be sure I am downstream.

I have been fortunate in doing all my fishing with three of the most delightful and generous hosts: Philip Martin on the Torridge at Beam, Johnny Collingwood on the Tweed at Cornhill, and Anne, Duchess of Westminster, on the Laxford.

Philip Martin, a really great fisherman, is more concerned that a friend should get a fish than about himself, and it was at Beam that I started. Incidentally, Beam is the home of Henry Williamson's famous Tarka the Otter—not that one sees otters there now: more likely, and unfortunately, mink. Philip had a great character as a gillie: Charlie Edworthy, aged over seventy, who had lived long on the river and knew everything about the fish, the birds and the flowers. A man of well over sixteen stone, he always had on a mass of clothes with a smart 'homburg' hat—on rough days he tied it on with a ribbon. Charlie never refused anything to eat or drink, he enjoyed a cigar, and when handing him my tobacco pouch I knew there would be little left: he had a pipe the size of an incinerator. On 11 March 1956 when fishing at the Sunken Tree, I landed my first fish. Charlie climbed down the wall and having landed my fish, a fifteen-pounder, he said, 'Well dun, sur, that's the firrst fish 'n' all my yearrs I've landed for a blind man!'

Until Charlie died we had many a happy day together, and I learned much, some of it not to be practised by 'fishermen'. One year on my birthday, Charlie said, 'Prahpurr, we muss getta fish t'day.' Off we went to the Sunken Tree. Having fished it with a fly and then spun without success, Charlie told me to stop. He must look at my minnow. There was much fiddling and then I cast. As I reeled in I felt a fish. It jumped high in the air and was gone. At the same moment Charlie hissed, 'Let ut zink!' Hell, I knew I was on the bottom. And then I heard the voice of the bailiff saying good morning. Charlie explained that I was stupid and had got on the bottom, he would have to go across river with my fly rod to cast across my line and pull me off. I sat down and talked to the bailiff. Later I realised I must have been fishing with an extra three hooks, or treble, fixed on behind the minnow!

Each year since 1957, Johnny Collingwood, who was at Sandhurst with me, later serving in the Queen's Bays, has asked me up to Cornhill. For six days I fish hard and I have been taught much by two of his boatmen, Charlie Young and Brian Turnbull. Wonderful days we've had together; but in February with ice on the river, Brian would tell me to hold the rod underwater to clear the rings, and sitting in the boat the soles of one's boots froze to the bottom. These were exciting days, for with the cold water the fish did not 'run'. I shall never forget one day, 26 February 1962, when we collected eight fish, a total of 81 lb. We sat in the boat in a blizzard, and when I got a fish I could hardly hold the rod I was so cold. On the bank I had to pass the rod to Brian while I swung my arms to get warm again, then back with the rod, with Brian breaking ice at the side to land the fish. How wonderful it all was: sometimes bitter cold, but then also the lovely spring days when the valley echoed to the call of the partridge or mallard.

Anne, Duchess of Westminster, known as Nancy to her friends, had been a great friend of my Victoria and they had got to know each other even better during the war, when a General driven by Nancy (a F.A.N.Y.) had come to see her. Great was the General's surprise when Victoria asked both him and his driver to supper, and Nancy, on this occasion, did not have to stay in the car or disappear to the kitchen.

I was thrilled, early in 1960, when Victoria received a letter from Nancy asking if I would like to go and stay, and fish on the Laxford. Fright overtook me for I'd hardly started fishing, and I little realised then how important a part these visits were to play in my life. The Laxford is possibly one of the best salmon rivers in the world. It is at the topmost corner of Sutherland, only about four miles long, and runs out of Loch Stack, overlooked by Ben Arkle and Ben Stack, into the Lax Fiord.

Although I'd never met Nancy I'd known her brother Adam Sullivan, who was tragically killed in the invasion of Norway in 1940. There could be no more sincere and generous friend than Nancy Westminster when times are difficult; I enjoy her enthusiasm and 'leg pulling', and her sense of humour guarantees that it doesn't matter whether I fish well or badly. It is hardly surprising that all who work for her are so loyal. The gillies are all supreme and I've been lucky to make such friends as Scobie, now over eighty but cheerful as ever, his son Billie, and Donald and Neil. All ready to encourage or rightly to tell me when I am quite useless. Scobie, with his 'That's no good. Wiggly wobbly. Wouldn't satisfy anyone.' And then, 'Ah, that's all right, on target.'

That first year, while we were there, the river was almost too low. One day with Neil Morrison we were fishing the pool near the sea known as Sparlings. I was casting away quite happily, when Neil suddenly left me and grabbed the net: with the low water, a fine salmon had been cast on the stones, coming into the pool, and Neil had him. The salmon was nicked in the mouth as if it had been hooked, and we returned triumphantly to the Lodge. When my fish was produced I was indeed the hero; Ronald and Lois Whineray, great friends of Nancy's and great fishermen, were amazed. I remained the hero of the day until the evening, when I told the truth. The Whinerays' day was to come. On the Saturday we left, the precious rain came, the river rose, and that evening Ronald and Lois caught sea trout to a total of 86 lb. Such is fishing.

Fortunately one remembers the unexpected great days of fishing and forgets the blank cold tedious days. That is as it should be, for the joy of fishing is the unexpected and unpredictable habits of the salmon.

Well do I remember one night, when Scobie had told me to tell Her Grace we were going fishing after dinner. We had dinner, and then I tentatively asked Nancy whether I might go with Scobie. It was a wild night and a Saturday, consequently we could only fish until midnight. After a second glass of port, and with Nancy telling me I was a fool, I changed into thick clothes and off I went with Scobie to the Sea Pool. Nearly every cast I made in the semi-darkness, something happened. Within an hour we'd landed about 33 lb. in weight; eight or ten sea trout. What a night we had, and I returned triumphant to a hot bath. As I put out my hand for the sponge a fish fell into the bath and another with the soap. I soon learnt that Nancy and Lois Whineray had lined the top of the bath with fish. These fish soon found their way into another abode.

The glory of fishing, I repeat, is that you never know what is going to happen. On 17 April 1965, on the River Torridge, for example. A sunny but cold day and truthfully I did not want to fish: the river was very low, almost no fish had recently been caught, and furthermore I'd been in London all the week and my back was giving me hell—lumbago, very painful, and perhaps too much port. Anyway, Victoria was determined that I should fish, for the good of my heath.

Jim Harding, a retired blacksmith, almost as blind as I am, although he still endeavours to do tapestry, arrived in his obsolete motor-car about nine-thirty and off we went—I secretly longing not to go, and wondering how early I could return. On arrival at Beam I was greeted by Philip, my as always optimistic host, assuring me there were fish about and I was sure to catch one. It surprised me that no one else happened to be fishing that day. Anyway, honour must be satisfied.

Jim Harding and I collected the rods, and off for a longish walk to the Yew Tree. Our friends the ravens were circling. The water was low, slightly coloured, and the sun very bright. I fished with a fly, but nothing. I then got out the spinning rod, all the time checking my watch—when could I go home with honour satisfied? By this time my back was giving me hell so I took some codeine. A pull, and I had something, difficult to gauge on account of the small rod. Eventually we landed a nice sea trout of about 3 lb. Perfect; now I could go home, and Victoria, as well as honour, would be satisfied. So off to luncheon in the hut, hot stew and beer. By this time my back had stopped hurting but I was pouring with sweat from the codeine. Philip came down, checked up on what I'd been doing and assured me I was certain to get a fish that afternoon. I was equally certain that with the low water and bright sun there wasn't a hope. And this is where fishing can be so wonderful: I was wrong.

Down to the Sunken Tree. I fished it down carefully with a fly. Not a movement. Then with my tiny 'yellow belly', right at the tail I thought I felt something. I fished the tail down again, but nothing. Jim said, 'One more for luck,' and possibly this was the first and last time an extra cast had luck: I felt something. Was it the bottom? And then the bottom began to move. I knew I had a fish but nothing showed, and I could do little with my small rod and reel which I couldn't really work.

It was a fish, and it cruised and cruised. Jim could see nothing as the sun on the water was so bright. (He never could see much, anyway.) After twenty minutes we were getting nowhere and I decided I must do something. I decided to hang on and walk backwards. Still the fish cruised. I kept on backing and suddenly Jim saw him and tried to get him, shouting excitedly, 'This is prahpurr! He's a monster. I've missed him!' At the same moment my reel fell off. I quickly got it back on again but in so doing twisted the line round the butt of the rod, which made the fish feel heavier than ever.

Thirty minutes had now passed and I was determined to get this fish, so I started to back again, calling to Jim to know if he could see it. By this time he'd got well out into the river—the fish splashed, and he was in Jim's net. Nineteen pounds—and now I could light my pipe. Well done, Jim.

But that wasn't the end. Oh no. On my host's instructions we must fish the 'Weir'. There I had to cast from the top of a wall some twelve feet above the river. Four casts and we were into another fish. Seemed heavy, but I still had my small rod with 9-lb. breaking-strength line. The fish became quiet, but to land it we had to get to the bottom of the pool, a hazardous walk of about fifty yards down a narrow path. Off we set, I with the rod,

Jim steering me, and fortunately that fish was docile. Slowly we worked our way down until, alas, Jim confided that we'd taken the wrong path. This meant a climb down a four-foot wall. Fortunately the fish decided to swim upstream, which was perfect, so away he went while Jim and I clambered down to the bottom of the pool.

Tim, my host's wife and her two grandsons, and an Australian friend had arrived with good advice. But the fish was sullen and not prepared to take any advice. After forty minutes I decided I'd had enough and come he must. After much pulling and praying, in he floated, and Jim had all eighteen pounds of him. What an afternoon—and that is fishing.

On Saturday, 8 April 1972, my superb gardener Keith, who gillies for me at home, was complaining about the Hell's Angels who'd done so much damage on Westward Ho! Golf Course. He told me that these blokes should have done National Service. I quickly said, 'But Keith, you have been with me five years and you have never done National Service.' To which Keith replied, 'Father says I've done National Service with you, Currnel!'

On Sunday the river was very high. Keith came with me and, expecting to fish from the bank, we both had short boots. All went well until I got into a fish and had to get to the water down a steep bank. 'Careful, Currnel. You'll be over your boots,' said Keith. Hell with my boots, I was up to my waist. As he stepped in, Keith said, 'This is my National Service!' And between us we had my 297th fish in the net. Then on May 14 Keith and I got my 300th salmon. Philip Martin, from whom I had learned and been given so much fishing, was, perhaps, even more pleased than I.

28

---◆·◆·◆---

A Colonel Again

No St Dunstaner who is asked about Lord Fraser would deny that we have been the best-trained and most hearteningly encouraged blind people we can imagine—though I shall never forget being asked to luncheon by Brigadier Critchley. He had suddenly lost his sight, and I arrived for luncheon with the intention of trying to inspire him and to assure him that he could still do things. When I enquired whether he had met Lord Fraser, the answer could hardly have been shorter. Yes. Lord Fraser had suggested so many things for him to take up that he'd had a heart attack.

But to me St Dunstan's has the traditions of a great regiment, and at times when I've been very down, I've only had to say 'Thank the Good Lord I am a St Dunstaner' to feel two or three inches taller.

Some years ago I went to a World Conference of War Blinded servicemen held in Germany. Each country in turn gave details of what was done for the 'War Blinded'. I sat next to a German officer, listening to what they did in Spain, Italy, France and the U.S.A. In Spain and Italy, if blinded in war, the man remained on full pay and received automatic promotion. My German friend whispered, 'You were in the wrong army. By now you would be a Field-Marshal in Italy or Spain.'

We hear much about the necessity of risk sports nowadays. A blinded person need not worry about these, for, if the challenge is accepted, his or her life is constantly a risk sport—even to finding the loo in a train or the right door to open when that train stops.

My son Nicholas had now moved to Germany with the Inniskillings and was soon encouraged to show-jump. In those days, the draw for Berlin competitions was done in alphabetical order, so his horse, Hans, unluckily always came after Halle, the Gold Medallist ridden by Hans Winkler. I expected Nicholas to remain in the Army but he decided instead to read Law at Cambridge. Having a year to wait, he went to Canada and got a job on Baffin Island. The place has a population of 287 and is frozen up for six months of the year. He and his mates, mostly French-Canadian, were flown in to Frobisher Bay where they were to build an air-strip. The work was hard, very long hours, and Nicholas has never earned so much money in his life. Sundays they fished for 'char', an arctic salmon. The Eskimoes used nylon washing-lines with large hooks attached, Nicholas a more sophisticated rod and spinning reel. Needless to say, the Eskimoes caught more fish.

All my children were enjoying life and doing well: much of that due to Victoria, who had been marvellous in a situation not unlike my mother's— who had to bring up Bunny and me after my father had been killed.

At this point in my life, when all my interests were spreading, my old friend, now General Sir Charles Keightley, asked me to take over as Colonel of the Inniskillings in 1957. Before the war that post had always been my ambition, and so the gesture meant a very great deal to me. But, I asked Victoria, could a blind man assume that position? Could he cope with inspections, the interviewing of suitable young officers, the taking of parades? One more challenge, and with Victoria's urging I decided I could do it.

Fortunately, on our first visit to the regiment, the C.O., Lt-Colonel Mike Tomkin asked Richard Keightley to steer me around, and brief me. Like his father, he left nothing to chance. Whether it was a parade, Church Service or even a reception, Richard Keightley 'walked' me through the lot. When nobody was about, I learned my directions, how many paces to take, when to acknowledge a salute. Thanks to Richard, it was fascinating how many people did not believe I was blind.

One morning I decided to have a quiet look around the men's barrack-rooms. They were very different to those of my day, when the troopers lived over the stables, for these rooms at Paderborn had been built just before the War for the German Armoured Regiments. Five or six men to a room, with baths and showers close by. Having had the room described to me by Richard, I went over to feel a bed. The one I chose seemed very hard, so I put my hand in to feel the mattress, and drew out a life-sized picture of an attractive young lady, almost in the nude. It was doubly funny, for obviously the Troop Sergeant, forgetting I couldn't see, had said when going his rounds that morning, 'Put that thing away, the Colonel might look in here.' Needless to say, we left it in its hiding-place and told no one.

It seemed nothing could escape the eagle eye of the Colonel. I'd been surprised to find our Band now carried a front line of side-drums, with smart banners, presented by General Sir John Anderson. I was inspecting the Band, and Mr Vince the Bandmaster was explaining all this to me, when, alas, I wanted to feel one of the drums, and, as luck would have it, chose the only one with a split skin. The Band had been playing in the rain the day before and there hadn't been time to change it. I feel sure Mr Vince was wishing I'd get my sight back—and not just for the usual humane reasons.

About this time Victoria became ill and had to go into hospital. The anguish and the many problems she had had to cope with since 1940 had finally taken their toll. Then she went to the West Indies for a holiday and during those two months I first learnt how lonely life could be. I gardened the more when at home, spending long hours in the potting-shed. It is a great advantage that one is able to pot up plants in the dark. And in the evenings I resumed the writing of the first part of this book. I'd always wished that my father had left a record of *his* early life: so I made three copies, one for each of the children. It was not to be published, I had no intention of that then, and the record was not to be seen until after I had left this world.

29

'This is Our Life'

Pillhead was seldom full now, with Antony serving in Cyprus, and Nicholas nearing the end of his time at Cambridge. Nicholas had done well at Magdalene, but like me had found time to hunt and race. He once rode in all five races at Cottenham, winning the first and going to hospital after the fifth! He became Master of the Cambridge Drag, and in order to have sufficient money for this he spent the summer working on the construction of the M1. His gang, led by a Polish foreman, consisted mainly of Irishmen who, when they found Nicholas was fond of racing, promoted him to driving a 'dumper'. Hard work, a ten-hour day or longer, seven days a week.

In March of that year, 1960, I was 'conned' into appearing on a comparatively new television programme, 'This is Your Life'. The B.B.C., having done much research, would lure the unsuspecting victim to the studio by some pretence, and before you knew where you were you were on the stage. In my case they'd asked Victoria, who was against it—after all, my life was our private affair. However, when they said that Antony would be given leave and flown home, she quickly changed her mind. A man arrived at Pillhead, and Victoria asked me to show him the garden. He asked many questions, and I was somewhat surprised by how little he knew, although he appeared to be interested in horticulture. After tea he left and I never gave it another thought, little realising that all my scrapbooks had gone to Bideford, where Mr Lee, my old sergeant-major, was carefully combing through the lot.

About a fortnight later, Peter Dimmock asked me to go down to the B.B.C. one evening with Bob Dean, to discuss a new television agreement. After a drink and settling our business, Peter explained that he would have to go. Everything had been carefully timed when, to Peter's horror, I asked where I might 'spend a penny'. This delay not only upset Peter but Eamonn Andrews, anxiously looking at his watch in the studio down the road. I wasn't best pleased, but all was forgiven when Antony appeared to say his piece. And great was Victoria's joy to have Antony home for a week, and at no cost.

Our riders were now steadily preparing for the Olympics in Rome. I'd been invited as a member of the Jury of Appeal under Prince Bernhard. I think the best part of this job was being given some excellent thin material for a suit, which when worn acted as a Passport.

I did not really enjoy the Rome Olympics, which were in fact to be my last. My old comrade Ranieri Campello, who had done so much for equestrian sport, had died after a heart attack the year before. We were at the Madrid Show when the wretched news was announced. And now the Olympics were becoming too large and spread out—one seemed to be for ever producing passports and identification cards. The equestrian events played a minor role, and there was a lurking suspicion, perhaps unworthy, that this was partly because neither the U.S.A. nor the U.S.S.R. saw much of an opportunity of gaining one more Gold Medal. As so often happens in sport, our Three-Day defenders of the 1956 Gold Medal seemed to have lapsed, but David Broome saved our honour by taking the Individual Bronze in Show-Jumping—in fact our only equestrian medal that year.

At home I was back to what we might term routine, with the two Shows and my 'Chairman' duties, ably assisted by George Worboys. At Pillhead I began to pull out of gardening, partly because I couldn't get staff, and when I came home at week-ends I didn't want to spend all the time doing accounts, or even bunching and packing endless snowdrops and daffodils. Antony had gone to South Australia in June as A.D.C. to the Governor, Sir Edric Bastyan; Nicholas had just come down from Cambridge with a good degree. We were well split up, and that possibly had something to do with my partial sense of anti-climax that year. It's a familiar state for parents whose children have spread their wings.

Victoria and I now wondered if Nicholas would become a barrister or a solicitor, and make money for the family. Neither in the event, for within a fortnight of leaving Cambridge he had married the daughter of Anthony and Vanda Taylor. This was delightful, for they had been great friends of mine for years—but what was Nicholas going to do now? He didn't keep us waiting long for the answer: he would return as a Regular to the Inniskillings. Victoria thought he was wasting his talents. Secretly, I was thrilled.

My term as Colonel of the Inniskillings came to an end in 1962. At the last parade, General Sir Charles Keightley, on behalf of Her Majesty the Queen, presented the regiment with a new Standard, and I was very moved when Charles and I inspected the regiment. And then Nicholas, in full dress, wearing my tunic and helmet, commanded the escort to the Standard during the Trooping. I don't know if one has to belong to an Army family to understand the peculiar pride such moments bring. On the Sunday following, my last as Colonel, they asked me to choose the hymns for the Church Service; among them I picked number 573, 'All things Bright and Beautiful'.

Victoria said it was a hymn for children; nevertheless we had it, and the troopers of my regiment sang it with huge gusto, children or not.

Now *all* my children had gone, at least temporarily. Antony in Australia, Nicholas married and in Germany, and Sarah elected to enrol at Perugia University to learn Italian.

At the end of 1963, Colonel Arne Franke of Sweden and I both decided to resign from the Bureau of the *Fédération Equestre Internationale*, in order to encourage new blood. We were made Members of Honour, which permitted us to attend meetings but not to vote. In actual fact, as so often happens, I found myself with more work as chairman of various sub-committees.

Nicholas was meanwhile back at Tidworth and beginning to be a good steeplechase rider. He took full advantage of being there and with his wife Viv's help, and very little money, collected three horses. In 1964 he won the Grand Military Gold Cup, on Threepwood. Victoria and I danced for joy. He was the first rider in over twenty-five years to have owned, trained and ridden the winner. How it recalled to me my endeavours to get a tiger. How much easier it is to achieve success if one has money. But how much happier one will always be to succeed by individual endeavour. And that Nicholas and Viv had done.

Early in that same year, I was asked by Admiral Sir Christopher Bonham Carter to come to Buckingham Palace to see Prince Philip. That evening Prince Philip asked me whether I thought it would be a good idea if he accepted an invitation to become President of the *Fédération Equestre Internationale*, when Prince Bernhard finished his term of office after the Tokyo Games. Without hesitation I said it would be a wonderful thing, and an inspiration to us all to do more. Prince Bernhard had competed, he knew too much, whereas Prince Philip had the advantage of not knowing all such technicalities as whether, for example, a rider should have a standing or running martingale. He left that to those of us who should know. When commanding a regiment, you listen to the signal officer, or to the medical officer, and then make your decision. And that is what Prince Philip did in the years to come.

Home from Australia, Antony joined the family brewery and became extremely interested in brewing, yet even more interested in a friend of Sarah's, Sue Liddell. So they married in October. Sarah herself didn't stay with the family like a Victorian daughter, neither did she take the now conventional path of becoming a secretary: as soon as she was old enough she joined B.O.A.C. as an air hostess. That job sounds glamorous to many, but it certainly isn't. She spent a couple of months learning First Aid, how to put out fires, and was even shot down into a swimming pool to cope with inflating a rubber dinghy. It all inevitably reminded me of joining the regiment—grooming, saddlery, sword drill and the forge. I'm glad to say that at the end of the course Sarah passed out top, receiving a silver ash-tray which remains forlorn because none of the family smokes. I was later fascinated to learn that the Senior Steward always looks at the passenger list, and then warns those under him of the more difficult regular passengers. I wondered if there might be any 'dossiers' on me. Nicholas and Antony had chosen most charming wives, and Victoria and I sometimes sat and wondered when Sarah would arrive with the milkman—to introduce a senior pilot or a very junior engineer.

The *Fédération Equestre Internationale* again occupied much of my time. Prince Philip gave me the job of chairing a committee to redraft the troublesome rules of Amateur and Professional. Fortunately I could count on Hans Winkler's advice. With all due respect to Hans, who is a great friend, he comes under the heading of 'brown' amateurs, but as Prince Philip so rightly said, 'Set a poacher to catch a poacher.' Between us we contrived what we consider a realistic definition: it hasn't yet been proved such, but the day will come when it will. More important to me on this committee, I was able to raise my old battle cry of encouraging large numbers of young riders, rather than dependence on a 'regular' team—which in the nature of things can only decline eventually. We emphasised the importance of the Nations Cup, devising a form of 'League' with a points system: the winners to be presented with the President's Trophy, a silver statuette of the Queen mounted, Trooping the Colour.

Naturally (or typically, my friends and enemies would say), having helped to make the rules, I was determined that Britain should win this trophy in the year of its inauguration. For this first year, with Harry Llewellyn's help, we planned as we might for any military campaign: a team to Nice and Rome, another to Madrid and Lisbon; yet another for Warsaw and Leipzig, returning via Aachen. All went as planned, although two gentlemen from the Foreign Office came to see me and asked if we would not send a team to Warsaw or Leipzig as it might upset West Germany. I'm afraid I said, 'Hell, we will go where we wish.'

We won in Warsaw, Leipzig and Aachen. The West Germans, like the Americans, applaud winners, so Great Britain was very popular. We won the President's Cup that year, deploying sixteen riders—and that was unrivalled by any other nation. And what an immaculate 'square' they formed at the Horse of the Year Show, on the last night's Cavalcade for 1966.

30

The Accolade

It had always been an intense desire that we should have a civilian 'Weedon', and around 1964, on the advice and instigation of Dorian Williams, it was hoped we might form an Equestrian Centre out of London. It's now sometimes forgotten that in the past those who organised and instructed in the horse world were usually officers and non-commissioned officers who had served in the 'horsed' regiments. These last, of course, no longer existed; hence it became the Societies' responsibility to train instructors. Thanks to Colonel Guy Cubitt, that was happening in the Pony Club, but not elsewhere. Dorian and Bob Dean visited Stoneleigh, and decided we might conceivably build offices and a riding school within the grounds of the 'Royal' (The Royal Agricultural Show). Once again, where was the money to come from? Philip Gell, more than anyone, convinced me that if we waited costs could only rise, so we went ahead. By 1967 the offices for both the British Horse Society and Show-Jumping Association had been built there, and the staff of the two London Horse Shows and I moved to Belgrave Square, together with Public Relations (Promotions they call it now). This was a very welcome turn of circumstances, for both Dorian Williams and Jack Webber took much off my back.

Since 1960 Victoria had not been well, and had been unable to accompany me on my various trips or to meetings abroad. In 1963 she'd been in hospital—TB was suspected—and now her throat was so bad that she had quite desperate difficulty in talking. Not being able to see her lips move, I didn't always know when she was speaking to me.

Victoria had always been critical of my interests and work being so much away from Devon, and Bideford in particular. It troubled me, but I just could not do more, although I would have liked to have been a councillor, particularly as Pillhead had belonged to the Stucleys who had done so much for the district. But in 1967 I became High Sheriff of Devon, the largest county in England after Yorkshire, and that made us both very proud. Now I badly needed my Victoria's help, but she had become dreadfully weak. The diagnosis of TB became suspect, and we wondered.

The duties of High Sheriff are in the main traditional, and thank heavens we still glory in our traditions. There were the Assizes, and though they fortunately didn't coincide with my two Shows, it all meant more work. At home, Victoria had to rest quite a lot, and owing to lack of staff, except for our dear 'daily', Mrs Cloak, I had to cope in the evenings. I became an adequate cook, and Victoria found my steamed turbot quite acceptable.

Before the first Assizes I, as always, went into every detail. After rehearsing the ritual at the 'Castle' in Exeter, we went to the Cathedral, and here again I learned exactly what would happen. On these occasions I try with all my heart and soul to behave so that people cannot tell that I'm blind. Just before the Assizes in March Victoria had again been very ill and had to go into Exeter for further tests. We went together to hear the result of these, and characteristically Victoria put very direct questions to the two doctors. They admitted she had cancer of the throat, but were sure it could be cured.

I discovered it had become the custom for the High Sheriff to invite guests to a luncheon, and then to attend the Assizes. I couldn't agree with this; it seemed repugnant, after a good luncheon, to listen to some wretched prisoner endeavouring to prove he was not guilty. Like all who are new to the courts, I was fascinated to see how we almost lean over backwards to give the defendant maximum opportunity to prove his innocence. And rightly. The tactics employed by the Queen's Counsels are fascinating in another way: e.g. wasting time to gain the opportunity of speaking after the luncheon break, or the next day. All these procedures intrigued me because in the Regiment I had served as 'Prisoner's Friend'—a culprit has the right to select an officer for this. The first time, I'd succeeded in getting a trooper acquitted: in the dark, when a bit drunk, he'd struck an N.C.O. of the Guard. For many moons afterwards every 'accused' chose me as his friend, until they eventually learnt that I wasn't always so successful.

My sister Bunny used to come down during Assizes to help me. Although Victoria was so ill, I shall never forget her spirit: she insisted on being present at the first Session to help me entertain the Mayor of Exeter, and immediately afterwards went to the nursing home to start the painful deep-ray treatment. In the long months to come it was a kind of relief to be able to talk about it, just as we had been matter-of-fact about my becoming blind. I think it helped her. When she returned from the Nuffield Nursing Home, although her voice was weak, we felt convinced she was cured.

Sometimes I think Sarah felt she should be at Pillhead looking after Victoria, and me—but I was determined it should not happen. I took pride in believing that I remained 'independent', and only later realised how wrong I was. Independent in getting around and keeping myself occupied, yes: but that is not independence. Now I know just how much I depended on Victoria for advice, encouragement and support at the critical times.

On 1 January 1968 I was knighted, and in March went with Victoria,

Nicholas and Antony to receive the 'accolade'. Mr Smith, the Queen's page, had been detailed to look after me. 'How many steps would I take . . . ? Then what should I do . . . ?' 'Turn left and take one step towards the Queen, kneel on one knee, to receive the touch of the Queen's sword on each shoulder.' We practised it over and over again, and although Mr Smith accompanied me I think I could have managed it alone. As I listened to the Queen, it was inevitably one of the most moving moments of my life.

That evening the whole family with their wives, and Bunny too, had dinner together in an excellent restaurant, Granny by Candlelight. I fear it no longer exists. Time the devourer of all things.

31

◄◄►►

Sunset 1969

As usual I'd attended the International Equestrian meeting in Brussels, in 1968, but had returned a day early. A short while later I received a note from Menten de Horne, Secretary General, telling me that Prince Philip and the Bureau had appointed me chairman of a committee to draw up rules for 'International Driving of teams of four horses'. I telephoned Menten: 'What's all this? I know nothing about driving.' I was told to draw up Rules for International Driving. When I enquired about the committee, the reply was 'Whomever you wish.' This last reply was the only one I really liked. Subsequently I spoke to Prince Philip on the telephone and explained that I knew nothing about driving—I could only presume I'd been given the job since I was not there to say, 'No, thank you.' He disagreed with that, and merely said I had been asked to do this because he *wanted it done quickly*.

So now it was to be 'Driving'. After I'd found out all I could by picking the experts' brains, I suddenly had the idea that it might be run as for a Three-Day Event: Dressage, Endurance, to be a Marathon, then Obstacle Driving equivalent to the Show-Jumping. Frank Haydon was most enthusiastic, and when I'd drafted the plan he came down to Pillhead. We started before dinner, and afterwards settled down to work through the night in this little room of mine. At 3.00 a.m. we had a bottle of champagne which got us through another hour, and then we'd finished. That is how I like to work. So many plans have been made in this study; it was just one more. The rules went to Prince Philip on a Friday, and were back on the Monday with suggestions and corrections in H.R.H.'s handwriting. I've often wondered how he gets through so much work on such a scale.

Up to that time Britain had taken little interest in competitive driving. Poland, Germany, Hungary, Switzerland and possibly Holland were the keenest, and so, accompanied by Frank Haydon and his German secretary, Anne Weber, I flew to Aachen to discuss these rules with experts of the interested nations. Heaven knows why they thought I was the 'King' of driving, and they told Frank how clever I was to bring 'my' secretary who spoke German so fluently. Frank didn't let on about either of their mistakes.

When the rules came into force in 1969, I'm perfectly certain my friends on the Continent could not have imagined that, three years later, in the World's Championships, Britain would win a Silver and Bronze in the Individual and Gold in the Team. Whether or not they still believe I know much about driving, I doubt.

The Olympics held in Mexico in 1968 were certainly a triumph for our horsemen: particularly the Three-Day Event Team. We had established a convincing lead in the Cross-Country, under terrible conditions, and about ten-thirty at night I telephoned Reuters from the Cavalry Club; I learnt that Derek Allhusen had won the Silver Individual, but nothing was in about the Team. A very large whisky and soda was called for, and we drank his Silver health. Then I went to bed to listen for the news. Yes, we'd won the Gold Team. So into a dressing-gown and down to the hall and another large whisky to celebrate. Back to bed, thanking the Good Lord, and I'd hardly got in when I was surprised to hear my telephone ring—surprised, because the Cavalry Club telephones are very antique and seldom work. I heard the night porter's voice saying, 'Colonel Sir Mike, you are wanted on the telephone.' 'By whom?' 'The Queen,' came the astounding reply. A good old leg-pull from downstairs, I thought, and was about to say, 'Bloody hell, I may look a fool, but I'm not having this one,' when Her Majesty's voice came through: 'Isn't this wonderful?' It *was* wonderful. My antique telephone cut us off, of course, as always, but fortunately Her Majesty came through again.

Hardly had I got over this when my overworked telephone managed to ring once more: Paul Fox, to ask if I would appear on television in the Olympic programme, at about 1.00 a.m. Thanks to those two very large whiskies and soda, I said I would come if the B.B.C. sent a car, and it was agreed. That splendid day fittingly ended with all the praise our riders and horses deserved.

In London I now had only the two shows and the advance H.Q., as it were, of the two horse societies. Thankfully that enabled me to spend more time at home, and I could in my turn try to be the encourager when Victoria, as she did, became depressed.

The garden was well reduced. I didn't bother about selling bedding plants any more; but still kept up the seed crops. Gradually we cleared undergrowth and nettles in the woodland around the house. I've already recounted how I enjoy this, partly because it is a good way for me to keep fit. With Keith's help, I would put down a long guide line and raise it about two feet above the ground, then set to swathed in mackintosh trousers and sweaters. Thus I managed to keep my weight within reason, and there's nothing like that kind of work to get one through difficult periods.

Major-General Roger Evans and his wife lived in Somerset, and although fairly close we seldom saw them. As I've written, I had served Roger Evans as adjutant and equitation officer, and had considerable admiration for both him and his much younger wife, Eileen. As adjutant I was regularly in and out of their house at Aldershot, and I taught Eileen to ride. Although the Colonel's wife, she attended riding school and joined in with the recruit rides. Victoria and I suspected that Sarah was fond of Sandy, their youngest son, and early in June Sarah came home with him. I was sitting here after tea, when he came in and rather nervously asked if he could have a drink, then further asked if he might marry Sarah. I was naturally delighted, but Victoria, being perhaps more old fashioned, fairly grilled him the following day as to whether or not he had the 'sufficient' to look after our daughter. The wedding was fixed for late November. Roger Evans died on October 23. Nevertheless, Eileen insisted that the wedding go on. It seemed a perfect marriage, and Victoria and I felt very fortunate.

During 1969, although Victoria lacked energy and her old enthusiasm, we believed or pretended to believe that she was cured. I had more or less decided to withdraw gradually from the horse world. We were coming up to the twenty-first Horse of the Year Show; more and more were riding; both my enterprises paid their way—surely I should retreat and enjoy myself with Victoria, live in the country, as I preferred?

On the evening of October 11, Victoria came to watch the Cavalcade of the twenty-first year; possibly our finest. The European Champion, David Broome, on Mr Softee; Pat Taaffe on Arkle, the greatest of all; Mary Gordon Watson on Cornishman. These three grouped under the centre light, and we were very moved when Ronnie Duncan's tribute to the horse was read. I had not missed a single performance during those triumphant years.

After a good rest on Sunday, October 12, my wife and I went to the Pool once again, but this time to enjoy ourselves without responsibility. Colonel Handler and the Spanish Riding School of Vienna executed their superb ballet for us.

On October 13 we had agreed that I should work in the morning, Victoria and Sarah would then meet me at the station. 'Home again, home again, home . . .' we always sang as we passed the white gate of Pillhead.

Early in the morning I packed, and had breakfast in our room. Victoria talked quietly, but did not want breakfast so early. I left, and later Sarah telephoned. She had arrived to help Victoria pack and found the door locked. She was getting the master key. She went in, and saw her mother sleeping. Victoria did not wake again. She died before I could get there.

32

Clouds and Eclipse

Here in this small room, where Victoria and I had discussed our worries and savoured our successes, here I could be alone, think and listen. Listen to the pigeons, the bees on a sunny day, and often rain on the conservatory roof. I think for the first time I felt truly blind. What was I to do? Victoria had seen me back into an energetic life, and, tired, had perhaps paid the penalty for the long years of responsibility. Now she had gone.

My friends left me to sort myself out, and of course I had been partly prepared for this disaster, as I had been for total blindness. My strangest sensation, which stirred old flickers of superstition, was pondering the fact that on two occasions when getting away from the 'horse', everything had gone wrong. In 1939 I left my job as Brigade Major to return to my Armoured Regiment. Now in 1969, about to withdraw from the horse world, Victoria had died.

My training counts for something, and I knew I must fight back. Now I had no choice but to return to the jobs that I can truly say I had done with some passion for all these years.

In January Eileen Evans came and stayed, and during 1970 we found that we'd become more and more fond of each other. We seemed to have the same thoughts, she had the same sense of humour as Victoria. Apart from having 'come out' at the same time, she and Victoria looked uncannily alike. There was hardly any point in avoiding what we meant to each other, and on 17 December 1970 we were married. Christmas that year was a very happy one, with the Evans and Ansell families even more closely united.

I was still potting up plants in the afternoons, when I wanted to listen to some football match on the radio; and raking up leaves; but now Eileen taught me a new occupation: appreciating and cleaning lovely furniture. Eileen had brought her furniture to make Pillhead even more perfect: mainly walnut of the Queen Anne period. I polished as I listened, alas, to Scotland defeating England at rugby football. I learned the importance of cleaning the beautiful handles and those awful claw feet. Then Eileen became keen

on fishing. She landed one for me at Beam in March and how happy we
were to have done it together. We did everything together and were never
separated. In June, Nancy Westminster allowed us to go to Stack Lodge,
Sutherland, to fish for a week, and there with Billie Scobie's help Eileen
got her first salmon—bigger than the one I caught—which gave her immense
pleasure. Life was perfect, or perhaps I should say almost so, for one day I
had my first ride since 1939. It will possibly be my last. For some years,
Nancy had been telling me of a fabulous loch, Loch Dionard, about ten
miles across the hills from Lochmore. I'd talked rather big about walking
there. Nancy had left instructions with Billie Scobie to make sure Eileen
and I went there during this short stay. She knew I would never walk it, so
kindly arranged that two ponies, Bella and Corry, would be shod ready to
take us.

Billie didn't like to disregard Her Grace's instructions, so one cold, snowy
day in June, Eileen and I, with Billie and two others, set out for Dionard.
Eileen mounted Bella, and I Corry. Riding up those steep tracks was frightening when one couldn't see. I just left it to Corry, hanging on with both hands
to the front arch of the saddle. Up we went to about fifteen hundred feet,
and then the descent. This was far worse. I could feel the sure-footed Corry
trying each boulder to see if it wobbled. I just sat and prayed. Down to the
many burns Corry scrambled, walked across, and with one bound was up
on the far bank. My problem was, when would that bound come? On
arrival at the end of the track, poor Billie had to pilot me on foot for half a
mile across bogs and deep ditches. Most of the way I went on my bottom.
I fear the fishing was hopeless: it was snowing and much too cold, but
quietly I was glad to have done it with Eileen. 'Father' Scobie merely thought
me a fool when I told him how frightened I'd been.

Then came the Royal International Horse Show. In August we had an
extra Show at Earls Court, and rather than go up to join Nancy at Lochmore
I knew I had to stay and help to organise it. Eileen remained with me, of
course, and after the three days we returned happily to Pillhead.

On Tuesday, August 31, Eileen was to take the car to London, packed
with all our fishing kit *en route* for Lochmore. Sandy would go with her to
drive some of the way, and Antony and I would go by train, meeting Eileen
that evening. How we both were longing for this visit to Nancy, and as
Eileen left at six-thirty in the morning, 'Drive carefully, darling,' I said. I
knew she would.

Sarah took Antony and me to Exeter. At Paddington I was met by John
Stevens, who has done so much for me as my number one, and I thought
he must have travelled up on the train with us. He had to tell me that Eileen
had met with a fatal accident.

They had stopped in Mere for breakfast. The first hotel was not open, and so they crossed the road to another. After breakfast, Eileen walked up on the pavement to buy some cigarettes. A lorry came downhill, the brakes failed, it skidded over the inch-high curb and across five feet of pavement. It had hit my Eileen.

33

I Follow the Drum

In the old days, all orders were given to our troops by the drums, long before bugle or trumpet calls became commonly used. That is what was meant by 'follow the drum'. I still do, for although a malign fortune destroyed my military life and has twice destroyed my private life, I still feel myself to be a soldier, think like one and try to act like one. But the circumstances of Eileen's death were such that my faith was shaken, and more than shaken. There is something in human nature which makes us imagine a kind of innate if not divine justice, and I had always believed, naively perhaps, that one's 'ups and downs' tended ultimately to balance. Now I felt how appallingly foolish it is to think of life as though it were an accountancy system.

My son, Nicholas, wrote straight to the point: 'Dad, since 1940 you have had thump after thump, and each time it takes longer to get back off the ropes; this last one was without the count.' During the next weeks while I tried to pull my mind into some kind of order, the Horse of the Year Show went on without me—as any good regiment should. The first show, or single performance indeed, I'd missed since the start in 1949.

What was I to do now? Either I must pack in—stay at home, see nobody, give up everything and perhaps 'take to the bottle'—or I must go on. I worked with something like frenzy at all the old odd jobs: potted up blue polyanthus by the hundred, ranged the garden finding leaves to rake up, and when the weather was bad I cleaned furniture harder than ever. At this last in particular I seemed to make a desperate effort to regain a grip, literally a grip, on reality. I would take one of the lovely pieces my Eileen had so recently brought into the house and clean and polish it until it shone. I knew it *must* shine, but one day the thought struck me, bitterly, that even if I could see I would only find my own image there. Thank God, I had many friends, three in particular, who sustained me.

By December I was back at work, helping to revise the rules for International Driving, attending the Bureau and General Assembly meetings. Three months later I was immensely proud to be given the Honorary Freedom of Bideford, a great honour, because I felt I'd done little for my home town, being so much away. In October 1972, Great Britain in the World's Championships held the Gold Medals in Show-Jumping, Three-Day Events and Driving. In the Olympic Games at Munich our Three-Day Event riders won the two Gold Medals and the Show-Jumpers won the Silver in the Individual.

I finish this story almost immediately after the Horse of the Year Show, the twenty-fourth at Wembley. It wasn't easy returning to my Club each evening: no Victoria, no Eileen, could say 'well done', or encourage when something had gone wrong. Yet almost to the point of fanaticism I became determined that this Show would be the best I had ever directed. If praise is reward, well, two people praised me in rather different ways. Night after night the 'House Full' signs were posted and I knew the 'touts' were out selling any ticket they could get hold of at a vastly increased price. I wanted to find out how they got them, so one evening I stood outside the main doors while a comparatively unknown steward (he'd just joined the team) wandered around enquiring the prices. Suddenly a chap came up to me and said, 'Guv, we all like you. Anything you put on is good, real good, and we both make money. Thank you, Guv. After all, Guv, you and I are the same, you're a sPIV like me, spelt the other way round!'

Walter Case, Editor of *Horse and Hound*, wrote of this show:

> Of all the previous 23 Horse of the Year Shows I have seen, none could equal that held last week at Wembley for its colour, artistry in presentation and, most important, its cliff-hanging excitement for the vast crowds which filled the Empire Pool every night . . . The Show Director, Colonel Sir Michael Ansell, had excelled himself. The architect of it all had staged a show to beat all shows and the general public owes him a tremendous debt for the immense pleasure it gave them.

Many would say, I wrote at the beginning, that I'd had more than a glimpse of fame and glory. But the iron fulcrum has turned my fate another way, and complete happiness eludes me. As I sit at my desk in this study, with the large Ilex tree outside and the smell of tobacco plants from the conservatory, when work is done I like to let my thoughts dwell on those things of which I am proud: commanding a regiment at an early age, polo with the Hurlingham team in America, representing Great Britain at Show-Jumping, and above all to have overcome blindness. If I were to look out west I would see beyond the lawn a few lights flickering from Bideford, a mile away, like coloured stars on a cold night; the sheep huddled and still; and in the middle of the field that lopped elm which has witnessed so much. A friend tells me I can't see them, but he is wrong, for in my mind I see things well. They blaze sometimes.

Index